RAHAB, HAGAR, & NAOMI

HOW THREE WOMEN OF THE BIBLE HELP YOU SEE YOURSELF THROUGH GOD'S EYES

BIBLE STUDY GUIDE | TWELVE SESSIONS

Jada Edwards, Nicole Johnson, and Kasey Van Norman

With Karen Lee-Thorp

Harper*Christian* Resources

Rahab, Hagar, and Naomi Bible Study Guide

Published by HarperChristian Resources, 3950 Sparks Drive SE, Suite 101, Grand Rapids, MI 49546, USA. HarperChristian Resources is a registered trademark of HarperCollins Christian Publishing, Inc.

Requests for information should be addressed to customercare@harpercollins.com.

ISBN 978-0-310-17967-2 (softcover)
ISBN 978-0-310-17968-9 (ebook)

HarperChristian Resources titles may be purchased in bulk for church, business, fundraising, or ministry use. For information, please email ResourceSpecialist@ChurchSource.com.

Published in association with the literary agency D.C. Jacobson &Associates, LLC, an Author Management Company, www.dcjacobson.com.

HarperCollins Publishers, Macken House, 39/40 Mayor Street Upper, Dublin 1, D01 C9W8, Ireland (https://www.harpercollins.com).

Art Direction: Ron Huizinga
Cover image: © LanaBrest/Shutterstock
Interior design: Denise Froehlich

First Printing August 2025 / Printed in the United States of America

Contents

How This Study *Works*

This study is for women who want to get into the real, messy parts of our lives that are usually under wraps. Through video teaching from a Bible teacher, a Christian counselor, and an actor playing out present-day dramas, we will first explore the human perspective from these three women, incredibly different yet so much like each of us—how each woman saw herself, how others saw her, as well as how we see ourselves in her story. We will also discover God's perspective: how he sees each of these women in Scripture and how he sees *us*.

We will find our own stories in the pages of Scripture.

Study Structure

Each session of the study will go like this:

CHECK IN. In Session 1 you'll introduce yourselves. In later sessions you'll have a chance to share something you discovered about yourself between sessions.

AT A GLANCE. This is a quick snapshot of an age-old problem we still deal with today, each biblical character's age-old solution or mistake, and a taste of God's wisdom on the subject.

VIDEO NOTES. Each video segment is 20–25 minutes long. It opens with a drama and then moves into a fast-paced teaching. This study guide contains space for you to take notes on what you see and hear in each video teaching.

GROUP DISCUSSION. The heart of the study is your conversation with the other women in your group. You'll be talking mainly about the real experiences of your lives. However, because this isn't group therapy, we strongly recommend that you commit yourself to the group ground rules discussed on the following page.

CLOSING PRAYER. End with your group leader or a volunteer reading aloud the prayer suggested in this section. Of course, any offered prayer is acceptable.

KEEP THIS CLOSE. These are a few short, memorable lines from the video that you may want to copy into your phone to go back to during the week.

ON YOUR OWN. Finally, you'll find activities to engage with on your own to carry your exploration of the topic deeper during the week.

- A Memory Verse to memorize over the course of studying each biblical woman
- In Real Life exercises to work through the dramatic interpretations each day
- Your Story to draw deep personal connections to the Bible
- Scripture Bible study to further marinate in each woman's story
- Journaling prompts
- Listening prayer activities

Do whichever of these activities you find helpful. Don't feel pressure to do more than you have time for. You'll have a chance to share something you got out of these activities when your group gathers the next time. You'll also have a chance to recite your memory verse together.

Group Ground Rules

This study gives you more of an opportunity to open up about your real life than most studies. You won't be pushed, but you will be invited to talk about how you see yourself and how you live. But your group is not a therapy session. It's not led by a counselor. If you need professional counseling or a forum to share the story of your past, ask your group leader or church leaders to recommend resources.

The following ground rules will help you stay on track. You should go over them in your first meeting to be sure that everyone understands and agrees.

CONFIDENTIALITY. Everything shared in the group must stay in the group. Don't repeat to outsiders what others share, even if you are all friends. If a group member misses a meeting, don't bring her up to date by sharing what others said in her absence. If something happens in the group that upsets you, don't discuss it with someone outside your group. Go to your group leader.

DISCLOSURE. This should be a safe place to tell the group the difficult truths of your past. However, the group does not need all the ugly details. Give your group the four- or five-sentence summary of your situation. If you need someone to hear the whole story, ask your group leader to help you get connected with a counselor. She can help you find the person on your church staff who has the names of counselors in your area.

TEARS. It's often good to cry when you share something hard. You're not embarrassing the group. If someone in your group cries, avoid words and actions that attempt to fix her sadness or solve her problem. Comfort is good; fixing is not. Don't let tears derail your time together. Keep going. The woman who has tears will be better sooner if the conversation carries on.

SHARED AIRTIME. Everyone in the group needs an equal chance to talk. Avoid telling long stories, especially about your past or about what you are struggling with today. If you have a lot on your mind that needs to be said, ask your group leader to help you get connected with a counselor.

PRESENT ORIENTATION. Naomi's past will come up in the study, and you'll have some time to think about your past. But for group discussion, concentrate on talking about who you are today, shaped by your past but not living in the past. Don't ask the group to sit through an account of what you went through. That's for counseling.

ADVICE. Avoid giving advice to other group members. If someone reveals a problem she is having and doesn't seem to know what to do about it, it can be tempting to suggest solutions. Avoid doing this. You can give her the gift of listening to her and accepting her as she is, and you can pray for her later on your own. Likewise, you should avoid asking the group to suggest solutions for situations you are facing. If you feel out of control and need help, ask your group leader to help you find a counselor.

What Materials Are Needed for a Successful Group?

- WiFi, Smart TV, monitor or screen for viewing
- One study guide for each group member
- Twelve-session DVD
- Bible(s) (at least one Bible to share for group time; each participant should have a personal Bible for in-between study time. If you need help resourcing Bibles, please email Eric.moreno@harpercollins.com.)
- Pen or pencil for each person during group time for notes

RAHAB

Don't Judge Me, God Says I'm *Qualified*

RAHAB
SESSION 1

Your Past Has a Purpose

Memory Verse

"Before I formed you in the womb I knew you,
before you were born I set you apart."

(Jeremiah 1:5 NIV)

Rahab DIDN'T LET HER **PAST** CONTROL HER **FUTURE** WITH **GOD**

Select a volunteer to read the following:

We all have a past. And not just any past, a past that is currently living and active—shaping the way we think, believe, and act right this very moment. How we remember our life determines not only the way we relate to ourselves and others but, more importantly, how we relate to God.

For example, some believe their backstory is too boring to be useful: relatively average, safe, no "traumatic" memories to speak of. From this vantage point, God looks more like a frail, old grandpa who would rather "bless our heart" than test us toward a life of suffering and sacrifice in his name. Or perhaps your past feels a bit too scandalous and sinful to be relevant in any plan involving holiness. From this angle, God looks more like a leather-wearing, skin-inked biker bully than an approachable friend who longs to satisfy your deepest desire.

If you feel unqualified to approach God or be used by him, join the club. The Bible is full of misfits who feel the same way. It is also a book brimming with the unchanging faithfulness of a God who gives meaning and purpose to both boring and scandalous people. In this study we're going to see the truth of this in action through the story of Rahab, a woman in the Bible who didn't let her past control her future with God.

Check In

Welcome to the first session of Rahab: Don't Judge Me, God Says I'm Qualified. To get started, give everyone a chance to do the following:

→ Say your name, unless everyone in the group knows you. Then, in three or four sentences, describe one of the places where you grew up.

Take a minute on your own to write down your response to this question (you won't have to share your answer):

→ How much do you believe God can work through you to accomplish his plan for good in the world? A lot? A little? What helps you believe that? What gets in the way?

At a Glance RAHAB

Where in Scripture: Joshua 2

Age-old problem: Being defined by your past and allowing it to determine your future

Rahab's solution: Take a risk, trust God, make a change

God's timeless wisdom: Everything that happens in our lives exists to make God more fully known to us and others. From horrific wounding at the hands of an abuser to marrying the love of our lives; from a monotonous nine-to-five job to beach sand melting between our toes. Nothing exists for its own sake. Everything exists for the sake of Christ: *"The Son is the image of the invisible God, the firstborn over all creation. For in him all things were created: things in heaven and on earth, visible and invisible, whether thrones or powers or rulers or authorities; all things have been created through him and for him." (Colossians 1:15–16 NIV)!*

Video Notes

Play the video segment for Session 1. It's about 23 minutes long, and you will be introduced to three speakers. As you watch, use the following outline to record thoughts that stand out to you.

DRAMA: Nicole

Reflecting on the shoes we've worn in our past can remind us of some of the most painful times in our lives.

There are plenty of shoes we never wanted to walk in.

TEACHING: Jada

Even if you feel stuck or defined by your old identity, God can re-identify you.

Sometimes you become a part of what your culture says is normal.

We all have religious frames of reference.

To be used on mission, all you have to do is open your heart.

TEACHING: *Kasey*

Sometimes you just need a little pressure to know there's another way.

Pressure points are the catalyst for change.

Somewhere along the way we have created our own version of the truth.

Our truth is designed to help us **survive**. *God's truth* is designed to help us **thrive**.

Thriving: Colossians 1:9–14

Rahab knows she needs deliverance, and she is desperate.

Group Discussion

Leader, read each numbered prompt to the group.

1 What stood out to you most from the video?

2 What is your honest, gut response to studying Rahab?

3 Our "truth" is a product of the experiences and environment in which we were brought up. What was one experience in your upbringing that made a big impression on you?

4 As a **child** we soak in the way people deal with conflict and love, or not. Share an example from your past.

5 As we move into **adolescence**, we decide if all of these core beliefs are true or false, based on the people around us. Share an example from your past.

6 In our **twenties**, we test-drive those beliefs. Share an example from your past.

7 In our **thirties and forties**, we may realize that there could be another way. Share an example from your past.

8 Think about your upbringing. Describe one way you learned to *give* love (such as cooking meals, giving gifts, spending time, working hard) and one way you were taught to *guard* love (such as expectations, busying yourself, resisting people's demands while avoiding direct confrontation, blame, isolation).

9 Is there an identity, name, pair of shoes, or label from your past that you feel stuck with or proud of? If so, what is it? Why does this identity make you feel stuck or proud? Discuss how you might overcome the label or identity.

10 Rahab was desperate for a new way of life. Are there things in your life that you are desperate to change? If so, what are they? Or if you have already made the change, how has your life been affected?

Select a volunteer
to read the following:

God designed us to be shaped by the experiences and environment in which we were brought up. Sadly, we all grew up in a broken world with parents who were broken to a greater or lesser degree. Their challenges affected us profoundly. It would be easy, then, to blame our parents and our society for the difficulties we face. But recognizing where our flaws may have come from doesn't take the sovereignty away from God, nor does it take the responsibility off of us. God wants us to come to grips with the way our past has affected us because he allowed it and intends to use it. We must choose to release our parents and society and learn over time better ways of seeing the world and relating to people. With God's help we can transcend our families and our society and actually contribute to making them better.

In preparation for the coming week, write one thing you want to gain from your study time:

(ex.: hope for my future, a better understanding of who I am . . .)

Closing Prayer

Ask for a volunteer to read this prayer aloud over the group:

Father God, you know everything about our pasts. Thank you for using all of our regrets, sin, failures, and inadequacies to remind us how desperate we are for a Savior. Thank you for using the best and worst parts, not in spite of us, but because of us. How grateful we are to be women, standing alongside our sister Rahab, qualified to take an active role in your eternal plan and purposes. Strengthen us this week as we open up more, and give us confidence to trust your plan. We pray in Jesus' name, amen.

Keep This Close

As you go on your way this week, here are some thoughts from the video that you may want to save in your phone or write on a sticky note so you can refer back to them:

- Our truth is designed to help us survive. God's truth is designed to help us thrive.
- Your past is a part of God's preparation so you can be a significant part of his plan.
- Even if you feel stuck or defined by your old identity, God has promised to use every part.

RAHAB
SESSION 1

On Your Own

Each session of this study also includes activities you can do each day between group meetings. These will help you gain a deeper understanding of both the Bible and how it relates to your personal life. **Don't feel you need to do all of these activities. Choose those that are helpful to you. The goal is to grow and develop a stronger relationship with God.** There will be time at the beginning of your next meeting to share whatever you've learned from these activities.

Memory Verse

"Before I formed you in the womb I knew you,
before you were born I set you apart."

(Jeremiah 1:5 NIV)

Memory Verse

There are many good techniques that may help you memorize Bible verses. Here are some of them:

1. *Write out the verse by hand on paper, along with its reference (in this case, Jeremiah 1:5). We remember as much as 80 percent more of what we write by hand than what we type electronically. That's because handwriting stimulates a more helpful part of the brain than typing does.*
2. *Even better, handwrite the verse and reference five times.*
3. *Read the verse aloud and act it out in an exaggerated way. Proclaim it dramatically. Actors have learned that the dramatic use of your body and voice will create associations in your brain.*
4. *Go for a walk and recite the verse and reference aloud. Walking increases memory formation.*
5. *Copy the verse and reference into your phone or onto a card you can keep with you.*
6. *Return to the verse three times a day to rehearse it. Say it aloud. Do this for all twelve weeks of this study.*

Learning the verse with its reference will help you find it in the Bible if you want to read the larger story around the verse.

We really hope you'll memorize this verse from the Bible. Committing verses to memory enables you to deeply internalize their truth and to have them with you when you need them. Here is the memory verse for Rahab again:

"Before I formed you in the womb I knew you,
before you were born I set you apart."

(JEREMIAH 1:5 NIV)

In this verse, God speaks to the young prophet Jeremiah and prepares him for the rough road ahead. He assures him that he, God, set him apart for service long before Jeremiah was aware of it. Everything that had already happened to Jeremiah was preparation for what God had made him for, and everything ahead was going to be woven into God's plan for the good of many people. God speaks these same words to you, because he has also set you apart for his service.

In Real Life:

DRAMA ACTIVITY: Shoes, Part 1

Little white patent leather shoes from age five and purple high tops from junior high remind Nicole of some of the most painful times of her life and the shoes she never wanted to walk in.

1 If you were going to tell a story about shoes (or some other artifact) that you didn't want to wear from your childhood, what would the shoes be? What is the story behind those shoes?

2 How did those shoes and that story affect the person you grew up to be? Do you still find yourself believing the story they told?

3 Have you ever worn shoes simply to "play a part"? If so, describe those shoes and why you wore them.

4 What would it look like to walk in your own shoes?

5 If God were to choose a pair of shoes for you, what do you think they would be like?

The Bible says this about what we wear:

Put on your new nature, and be renewed as you learn to know your Creator and become like him. In this new life, it doesn't matter if you are a Jew or a Gentile, circumcised or uncircumcised, barbaric, uncivilized, slave, or free. Christ is all that matters, and he lives in all of us.

(Colossians 3:10–11 NLT)

6 What do you think it means to become like your Creator? How do you suppose it's different from becoming like the "good church girls" you have seen or like whoever else you have tried to live up to?

7 How does it help you to know that it doesn't matter if you are "barbaric, uncivilized, slave, or free" (Colossians 3:11)? The Message translation of this verse may be a bit clearer: "Words like Jewish and non-Jewish, religious and irreligious, insider and outsider, uncivilized and uncouth, slave and free, mean nothing." What other things do you suppose don't matter?

Jesus also says:

"Walk with me and work with me—watch how I do it. Learn the unforced rhythms of grace. I won't lay anything heavy or ill-fitting on you. Keep company with me and you'll learn to live freely and lightly."

(Matthew 11:29–30 MSG)

8 What in this passage appeals to you? Why?

9 What is the hard part of doing what Jesus says here?

10 What are you going to do differently in your day-to-day life as a result of this exercise?

Rahab in the Bible

SCRIPTURE ACTIVITY

Look up Joshua 2:1–21 and read it.

The Old Testament tells the story of how God chose the family of Abraham to be his means of restoring the whole world to a relationship with himself. The family became known as the Israelites, and God promised to give them the land of Canaan as their homeland. He told them to drive out the Canaanites, whose culture was riddled with injustices like child sacrifice and ritual prostitution.

The Israelite army's first task was to conquer the walled city of Jericho. The general sent two spies into Jericho to assess the city's defenses. But no matter how well they dressed as Canaanites and spoke the language, their accents would give them away as foreigners. So they went to a house that served as a brothel, a likely place for travelers, that happened to be built on top of the extremely wide city wall. This was the house of Rahab.

1 Did Rahab make a deal with the spies before or after she hid them and lied to the king's men? Why is this significant? What does it tell you about her?

(NOTE: Many people dispute whether or not Rahab's lie was justified. Yet this imperfect part of her was still used by God for his plan. When your good intentions fall short of God's perfection, he'll still use you for his purpose.)

2 What reasons does she give for why she hid the spies? What does this tell you about her?

3 How would you describe her faith at this point? For example, what does she believe? Who does she trust, and why? What action is she willing to take to express her faith?

4 How is it significant that Rahab asks the spies to save her extended family, not just her as an individual? What does that say about her?

5 How would you describe Rahab's attitude toward her past in terms of moving forward with her future?

Personal Timeline

0 Birth

10 Pre-Teen/Adolescence

15 Teens

CONNECTION ACTIVITY

1. Complete a timeline of your life from childhood to age 25 (or to your current age if you're under 25). Note the key people and experiences.
2. Now take some time to write. How did those people and experiences help to shape the person you grew up to be? Use extra paper if necessary.
3. On the timeline, circle any season, choice, or experience that you think disqualifies you from being part of God's people and his mission to the world. Then take some time to pray for God's perspective on your past.

20 Early twenties

25 Late twenties

Journal Time

Choose *one* of the following topics to journal about:

- God met Rahab exactly where she was, using the most broken and messed up parts of her to get her attention. He does the same for you. What are the most broken and messed up parts of you? Maybe they're hidden so nobody sees them. Maybe you don't look at them yourself. But take some time now to look at your past and your present, and the things you do to survive. Write the truth of these things here. Then write about how God has used, is using, or can use these things to get your attention.
- Pressure points tell us things can no longer be the way they have been. What pressure point in your life is pushing you to make a change? What needs to change? How are you responding? What do you think would be the best possible response you could make? What is the hardest part about doing that?
- Which specific memories from your past tempt you to disbelieve God in your present? Which memories encourage you to believe him more than you have before?

Whichever topic you choose, finish up by writing about this question:

- What will you do differently in your day-to-day life as a result of this reflection? Again, use extra paper if necessary.

Listening

PRAYER ACTIVITY

God speaks to the heart—the core of you, where your thoughts, emotions, desires, motives, and choices come from. Take some time now to let him speak to you. Find a quiet place where you can be alone. Turn off your phone—or better still, leave it somewhere else so it doesn't draw your eye and your thoughts. Lay before God your thoughts about your past and any doubts you have about whether he can work through you. Then let the busyness of your thoughts go. If you find your mind drifting, just bring it gently back with a calm thought like *Speak, Lord. Your servant is listening.*

If you find you're easily distracted or struggling to find downtime in your life, try reading Psalm 139, and listen to what God is saying to you there. God speaks to us in his Spirit. The Spirit is activated through the stimulus of truth. Don't be discouraged if you don't hear an audible message from God. He is always speaking to you through his Holy Word.

Sometimes it helps to read aloud or change up your surroundings. Take a walk, sit on the porch, head to the nearest park bench, or simply sit in your car alone for a few minutes if necessary.

RAHAB
SESSION 2

Liking Your Reflection

Memory Verse

"Before I formed you in the womb I knew you,
before you were born I set you apart."

(Jeremiah 1:5 NIV)

Select a volunteer

to read the following:

Who do *you* see when you look in the mirror? Do you see a woman who owns her past or feels defeated by it? A woman who welcomes conviction or lingers in condemnation? A victor or a victim?

If we are honest, most of us see some of both depending on the day. Rahab would live victoriously in God, but like all of us who are brave enough to look in the mirror, she would first need to reflect on the very real wounding she experienced over the course of her life. We all have wounding.

In Rahab's case, she was a prostitute, using her body to survive, treating love as something to be bought and sold. She had years of patterns built up to protect her heart from hurt. We may never have been literal prostitutes, yet we all have patterns of thought and behavior that we created to survive but that block us from giving and receiving love as we were designed to do.

In this session we'll consider what can happen when we start letting go of those habits of self-protection and unforgiveness.

Check In

Before you dive into the video, take a few minutes to check in with each other. Let each person choose one of the following questions to respond to:

- What did you get out of the "On Your Own" activities you did for Session 1?
- How were you or weren't you shown love as a child? Please keep your answer under two minutes.

Next, say your memory verse aloud together. Be sure to say the verse reference after it. If you don't know the verse from memory yet, read it with the group from page 37.

Video Notes

Play the video segment for Session 2. It's about 18 minutes long. As you watch, use the following outline to record thoughts that stand out to you.

DRAMA: Nicole

We can easily begin to keep score with or rate other people. God does not keep score.

At a Glance: RAHAB

Age-old problem: Being hurt by others

Age-old mistake: Building walls of self-protection

God's timeless wisdom: As we grow increasingly secure in God's love, we will increasingly tear down the walls of self-protection: *And may you have the power to understand, as all God's people should, how wide, how long, how high, and how deep his love is. May you experience the love of Christ, though it is too great to understand fully. Then you will be made complete with all the fullness of life and power that comes from God (Ephesians 3:18–19 NLT).*

TEACHING: *Kasey*

Love as a commodity.

The more hurt we are, the deeper debts go, blocking the free flow of love.

There is no room for unconditional love in our life when we're hanging onto debts.

Colossians 2:13–14

> The love that God offers us is a love without condition, a love that requires nothing from us.

Group Discussion

Leader, read each numbered prompt to the group.

1 What stood out to you most from the video?

2 Kasey said, "All I had learned throughout my childhood, my teen years, and my twenties was that love was something that could be earned, that there was a price tag on it, that it was a commodity. I learned to exchange it, to give it only when I got something in return, and to return it only when someone needed nothing from me."

Can you identify with treating love as a commodity to be earned and traded for other things you want? Or have you learned to give and receive unconditional love? Describe how you deal with love.

3 What kinds of things do people trade for love?

4 How do we use our femininity to get what we want? Give some examples.

5 Think about Rahab's situation as a prostitute in her culture. Why do you think she had to wall off her emotions and eradicate her need for love in order to survive?

6 One of the things we do when we have been hurt and haven't forgiven is come up with strategies to protect ourselves from being hurt again. One strategy Kasey named is keeping emotional distance from others, not letting them get close to our honest, vulnerable parts. How might we go about keeping emotional distance from others? What behaviors might that involve?

7 What are some of the unintended consequences of keeping others at a distance?

8 Given that not forgiving others causes us problems, it might seem that the simple solution is to forgive them. But forgiveness is often hard. What do you think holds us back from letting others off the hook for what we feel they owe us?

9 Colossians 2:14 says that God has canceled the debt we owe to him. Does that make it easier for you to cancel the debts that others owe you? Why or why not?

10 God loves us without needing anything from us and without our having to return his love adequately. Have you experienced that love? If so, give an example of how you have experienced it. If not, how do you respond to the idea of it?

Select a volunteer
to read the following:

We see ourselves as vulnerable and in need of protection. We also believe that it's up to us to protect ourselves, or possibly to get somebody else to protect us. So we read with incomprehension the words and actions of Jesus, such as these:

> *"But I say to you who hear, Love your enemies, do good to those who hate you, bless those who curse you, pray for those who abuse you. To one who strikes you on the cheek, offer the other also, and from one who takes away your cloak do not withhold your tunic either. Give to everyone who begs from you, and from one who takes away your goods do not demand them back. . . . If you love those who love you, what benefit is that to you? For even sinners love those who love them." (Luke 6:27–30, 32 ESV)*

Jesus thinks it's up to God to protect us. He knows God won't protect us from all hurt, but he views hurt as not disastrous because he knows God will be with us in our hurt. Hurt can't destroy us as long as we're reliant on God. This is what helps him forgive quickly and cleanly, and to extend love to those who hurt him.

In preparation for the coming week, write one thing you want to gain from your study time:

(ex.: hope for my future, a better understanding of who I am . . .)

Closing Prayer

Ask for a volunteer to read this prayer aloud over the group:

Jesus, you know all the things we have done to others that make us feel that we owe them. You know all that others have done to us that make us feel that they owe us. And you know the many ways we have built up debt against you by not loving and honoring you as you deserve and by not treating the people you created as you wanted them to be treated. Yet you came to earth to pay for our debts against you. If we accept that generosity, we owe you nothing but gratitude. Please help each one of us experience your unconditional love and be changed by it. Please help us forgive and let go of our grip on our strategies of self-protection. We want to be able to love. We pray in your name, amen.

Keep This Close

As you go on your way this week, here are some thoughts from the video that you may want to save in your phone or write on a sticky note so you can refer back to them:

- The extent of our self-protection is directly correlated to the amount of unforgiveness or resentment built up in our hearts.
- Self-protection has unintended consequences that block us from giving and receiving love.

RAHAB
SESSION 2

On Your Own

Memory Verse

"Before I formed you in the womb I knew you,
before you were born I set you apart."

(Jeremiah 1:5 NIV)

In Real Life:

DRAMA ACTIVITY: Keeping Score

Nicole plays Susan, the daughter of an investment banker. Growing up, Susan got affection from her father when the market was up but withdrawal when the market was down. Susan learned to feel that she was a stock whose value went up or down depending on what she did. She began keeping score on herself in a journal, and eventually she started keeping score on other people. Finally, a friend accidentally picked up and read part of her journal and challenged her thinking about it.

1 Do you keep score on yourself? If so, what gives you a higher score?

What gives you a lower score?

Where does your rating system come from?

How does keeping score affect what you do?

2 Do you keep score on other people? If so, what gives them a higher or lower score?

How does keeping score affect the way you relate to them?

3 How many times this week have you lied on Facebook or purposely posted on Instagram just chasing the fulfillment of what others might think?

When you do that, how do you end up feeling?

How is your social media presentation of yourself different from the whole story about you?

4 Do you think other people lie on social media to impress readers? How does that affect the way you think about, feel about, and respond to their posts?

5 If you were going to create the most honest social media profile ever, what would you say?

6 Susan's friend says God doesn't keep score. Do you believe that deep down? What persuades you to believe it or not believe it?

7 The best way to know whether God keeps score is to sit down and read through an account of Jesus' ministry and see how he operated. You might start with Luke chapter 4 and read through to the end of the book. If you don't have time for that right now, here are some shorter passages, some printed out for you and others that you can look up. What does each of them say related to the topic of whether God keeps score?

Matthew 18:21–22

Luke 6:37–38

[Love] keeps no record of being wronged. (1 Corinthians 13:5 NLT)

Salvation is not a reward for the good things we have done, so none of us can boast about it. (Ephesians 2:9 NLT)

Luke 7:36–50

Your Story

CONNECTION ACTIVITY

Kasey said, "You can know that you have some debt to deal with in your life anywhere you are watering down your story, anywhere you are hiding out from the things that have really happened to you."

What parts of your story do you water down or exaggerate? In what specific groups of people do you most often do this?

Sometimes hiding out goes beyond watering something down. It can mean not telling anyone about it at all. You know you're doing this if you have never told anyone the story. You especially know if you have been lying to yourself about the story, saying it never happened, changing what really happened to something better, or putting up walls to avoid thinking about it. If you tell yourself, "That's in the past; I don't go there," you are hiding out. Chances are high that it is still affecting who you are in the present: what you choose to do and not do; how close you let people come. It may be fueling coping strategies that numb your feelings, strategies like staying constantly busy, compulsively checking your phone, living on social media, binge eating, or shopping with money you don't really have.

What is that story you are hiding from? What is that moment, that experience, those events, that hurt? Is there anybody in your life you can imagine telling the story to? If not, consider making an appointment with a professional counselor.

Or, begin by writing about the story. Write as much as you can about what happened. You can write it somewhere other than this book if you want to keep it secure. Writing can help you untangle the story you have been telling yourself from the story of what really happened. It can help you understand bits that haven't made sense. You may see that what happened wasn't your fault. You can set boundaries around the writing, like telling yourself you only have to write for ten minutes and then you can stop and do something good for yourself.

Don't want to write about it? Make a drawing. Draw some detail that sticks in your mind, like the orange bedspread. Or draw the room. Or draw an abstract picture of the feeling that goes with the experience.

Rahab in the Bible

SCRIPTURE ACTIVITY

Look up Joshua 6:1-25 and read it.

1 What do you think might have been going through Rahab's mind as the events of verses 8-14 took place? Remember that she didn't know what God had told Joshua.

2 What might Rahab have learned about God from watching the city walls collapse without the Israelites attacking them?

3 In verses 22-23, Rahab and her family were rescued. How might that have affected her relationship with God? What might she have believed about God then?

4 For the rest of her life, Rahab knew she was noticed by God. What she had witnessed could have left her hopeless, but it didn't. She knew that she would have a different experience of life going forward, and that

God was for her and not against her. How do you think knowing those things would affect the way a person feels and acts in life?

5 Do you know you are noticed by God? Do you know he is for you, not against you? How do you want your life to be affected by knowing that?

Journal Time

Choose *one* of the following topics to journal about:

- What is the difference between unconditional and conditional love? What experience have you had of unconditional love, if any? How has it affected the way you feel, the way you think, the way you act? Or if you can't remember ever experiencing unconditional love, how has that affected you?
- Are you secretly holding out for an apology or acknowledgment of offense from someone? If so, how do you think receiving this would help you? How have you been living with this offense without an apology since it happened? What would it cost you to forgive this person, to cancel their debt? What is not forgiving them costing you?
- Do you find yourself sabotaging relationships the closer they get? If so, what scares you most about the commitment and vulnerability required for godly friendship? Where do you think that fear comes from?

Whichever topic you choose, finish up by writing about this question:

- What will you do differently in your day-to-day life as a result of this reflection? Again, use extra paper if needed.

Listening

PRAYER ACTIVITY

Have a dialogue with God about love. Tell him what you have been settling for apart from him, and ask him for whole, eternal, and unconditional love. Ask for the kind of love that cancels your debts and leaves you with a clean slate. Open yourself to receive it. Talk with him about what it's like for you to do that. If you're afraid of him for any reason, tell him about that, and ask him to help you entrust your fear to him.

RAHAB
SESSION 3

What's in a Reputation?

Memory Verse

"Before I formed you in the womb I knew you,
before you were born I set you apart."

(Jeremiah 1:5 NIV)

Select a volunteer
to read the following:

Rahab had a complicated past. Really complicated. She carried wounds that affected how well she was able to give and receive love. But the downsides of her life were far from the whole story with her. God had made her with some unique qualities that equipped her to act effectively for him when the Israelite spies came to her door. He knew her long before this incident, and he had shaped her from before birth to be the woman he had planned for her to be. When he looked at her, he saw her wounds, but he also saw her strengths. These were qualities she was going to carry forward into her new life as his follower, and they would equip her to continue to serve him effectively.

In this study you're going to reflect on your own God-given personality and consider what strengths you have that equip you to serve him. Some of us have a much easier time seeing our deficits than our strengths, and that's where your group comes in: Even if they have known you for only a couple of weeks, they may already be able to see some of the things about you that you can't see. God has purposes and goals for your life. The more you seek him, the more you'll become aware of what those are.

Check In

Before you dive into the video, take a few minutes to check in with each other. Give everyone a chance to respond to the following questions:

- What did you get out of the "On Your Own" activities you did for Session 2?
- What is one positive personality trait you have?

Next, say your memory verse aloud together. Be sure to say the verse reference with it.

At a Glance RAHAB

Age-old problem: Having a complicated personality

Age-old mistake: Feeling like we don't fit in

God's timeless wisdom: God made us the way we are, and he will use us with the personality we have: *Your eyes saw my unformed body; all the days ordained for me were written in your book before one of them came to be (Psalm 139:16 NIV).*

Video Notes

Play the video segment for Session 3. It's about 20 minutes long. As you watch, use the following outline to record thoughts that stand out to you.

DRAMA: Nicole

What would Rahab have posted?

TEACHING: Jada

Rahab was bold and smart and strategic.

Whoever you are today is who God is going to use.

Joshua 2:9–11

When you observe the greatness of God, you melt, you submit.

The Proverbs 31 woman

Psalm 139:13

Be the best version of yourself.

Group Discussion

Leader, read each numbered prompt to the group.

1 What stood out to you most from the video?

2 How did Jada's description of Rahab's personality fit with a person who (according to Kasey in Session 2) had been hurt and was treating love as a commodity? Is it possible to be both?

3 If Rahab had had a social media account, what else do you think she would have posted?

4 How does it affect you to think of Rahab having qualities of the Proverbs 31 woman?

5 How would you describe your personality? How do you think God sees you? If it's hard for you to come up with words that describe you, you can scan the list of words under "Journal Time" on page 78.

6 How are you like Rahab? How are you different?

7 How can God use someone like you for his purposes?

Whoever you are today is who GOD is going to use.

8 What aspects of your personality and character do you think God wants to change? What aspects do you think he wants to keep as they are?

9 How easy is it for you to celebrate the way God made you? Why is that the case?

10 Rahab had the label "prostitute." But she didn't let it keep her from taking effective action or from moving toward God. Do you have a label or reputation that has been holding you back from embracing the way God sees you? If so, how can you begin to move past it and into who God says you are?

11 Rahab's heart melted when she heard about the greatness of God (Joshua 2:9–11). What has made your heart melt? How has that affected your choices?

Select a volunteer
to read the following:

One reason it helps to think of Rahab as a Proverbs 31 woman is that it dispels myths about that chapter of the Bible. For example, the chapter isn't a checklist that we are expected to live up to completely. It portrays an ideal woman, and even brand-new believer Rahab was living up to some of her qualities. Rahab wasn't married. She didn't have children. She had a couple of jobs and was supporting a family. She was damaged in some significant ways. And she had a lot to offer. We need to avoid looking at Proverbs 31 as a checklist of how we fall short of God's expectations. He made us the way we are, even if we never get up "while it is still night" (Proverbs 31:15 NIV).

In preparation for the coming week, write one thing you want to gain from your study time:

(ex.: hope for my future, a better understanding of who I am . . .)

Closing Prayer

Ask for a volunteer to read this prayer aloud over the group:

God, you made each one of us with our unique personality. Please help us to see and value the strengths you have given us. Show us how we can use them to do things in the world that you have purposed in us from before time began. We are grateful that even though you don't need us, you want us—that you desire to partner with us in accomplishing good things in the world. Please bring good even out of the aspects of ourselves that we perceive as weaknesses, revealing your strength in our weakness. Speak humility into our hearts and melt any part of our personalities we are clinging to more than you. Convict us—help us change. May we be women who see and affirm what is valuable in one another: celebrating instead of comparing, encouraging instead of criticizing. We ask these things in Jesus' name, amen.

Keep This Close

As you go on your way this week, here are some thoughts from the video that you may want to save in your phone or write on a sticky note so you can refer back to them:

- Whoever you are today is who God is going to use.
- When you observe, even indirectly, the greatness of God, your heart has but one response: to melt, to bow down, to submit yourself to the one true living God.
- Don't spend your time trying to be some sad version of someone else when all you need to do is be the best version of yourself.

RAHAB
SESSION 3

On Your Own

Memory Verse

"Before I formed you in the womb I knew you,
before you were born I set you apart."

(Jeremiah 1:5 NIV)

In Real Life:

DRAMA ACTIVITY: Social Media Posts

1 Nicole speculated on some of the posts Rahab might have made if she'd had social media. You had a little time in the group meeting to share your ideas for posts, but now think a little deeper. Look again at Joshua 2 if it's helpful. What might have been some of Rahab's posts . . .

- before the spies came to Jericho, when the rumors about the Israelites were flying around town?

- after the spies left her house, during the weeks when she was waiting for the Israelites to return?

- after the Israelites destroyed Jericho, and she was getting used to her new life?

2 What might she post if she observed life in your world today? Think about how her personality would react to your life and the world you live in.

3 What kind of person are you on social media? How are you like or unlike the way you are in real life? If you're not sure, go back and read some old posts as if they were posted by someone else. What kind of person do you see?

4 What kind of a person would you like to be on social media? Why?

5 Read Colossians 3:12–15. What is hard about living this way on social media? Write down the qualities that are especially hard.

Why do you suppose these qualities are so hard to practice on social media?

6 Verse 12 says one thing that helps us develop these qualities is reminding ourselves that we are God's chosen ones, holy and beloved. Do you think of yourself as chosen? What about beloved? What helps you or gets in the way of believing this?

7 How do you think taking this on as part of your identity could help you on social media?

8 What are you going to do differently in your day-to-day life as a result of this exercise?

Rahab in the Bible

SCRIPTURE ACTIVITY

Look up Matthew 1:1–6 and read it.

Rahab is mentioned three times in the New Testament. The first time is right at the beginning, in the first chapter of Matthew, a genealogy of Jesus that lots of readers skip over.

1 This genealogy (which continues through verse 16) mainly mentions Jesus' male ancestors, but these opening verses mention four of the women who were his foremothers. Does it surprise you that Rahab is highlighted in Jesus' family line (verse 5), even though she was a prostitute and a non-Israelite? What does this say about the message of this genealogy?

2 The other three women mentioned in these verses are:

- Tamar (verse 3). She was Judah's daughter-in-law, but her husband and Judah's second son died. By law Judah should have married her to his third son so she could have children in her late husband's family line, but Judah was afraid she was a curse on the family, so he let her languish. To get her rights, Tamar disguised herself as a prostitute and seduced Judah. When she became pregnant, she produced proof that she wasn't just sleeping around and that Judah was the father. Thus she secured her place in the family (Genesis 38). This is how Perez was born and got into Jesus' family line.

- Ruth (verse 5). She was an impeccably virtuous woman but from a hated foreign country, Moab. The law said, *"No Ammonite or Moabite or any of their descendants may enter the assembly of the LORD, not even in the tenth generation" (Deuteronomy 23:3 NIV).* Yet a good Israelite named Boaz married her, and she was welcomed into his clan, and her great-grandson David was anointed as king of Israel.
- Bathsheba ("Uriah's wife," verse 6). Matthew makes a point of saying that before she was King David's wife, she was Uriah's wife. David seduced her, and then when she got pregnant he had Uriah murdered so he could marry her (2 Samuel 11).

Why do you think Matthew included the names of these women in Jesus' genealogy? What do you think he was trying to say by including them?

3 How does it affect you to think of Jesus with these women highlighted in his family line?

Hebrews 11 gives a long catalog of Old Testament people who lived by faith. The list is intended to encourage readers to live by faith too. Read the following excerpts from this chapter:

> *1 Now faith is confidence in what we hope for and assurance about what we do not see. 2 This is what the ancients were commended for. . . .*
>
> *6 And without faith it is impossible to please God, because anyone who comes to him must believe that he exists and that he rewards those who earnestly seek him. . . .*
>
> *31 By faith the prostitute Rahab, because she welcomed the spies, was not killed with those who were disobedient. . . .*
>
> *39 These were all commended for their faith, yet none of them received what had been promised, 40 since God had planned something better for us so that only together with us would they be made perfect. (Hebrews 11:1–2, 6, 31, 39–40 NIV)*

4 The writer defines the word *faith* in verse 1. How did Rahab show confidence in what she hoped for? What did she hope for? (You can look back at Joshua 2.)

How did she show assurance in what she didn't see?

5 How is this kind of faith different from simply believing a set of facts about God?

How is it different from self-confidence, or confidence in the universe?

6 Verse 6 says, "Without faith it is impossible to please God." Why is that the case?

What are the implications of this fact for us?

7 Verses 39–40 say that Rahab (and the other people listed in the chapter) didn't receive what God had promised. That was because she and the others were waiting for something more than they ever experienced in their lifetimes, something God fulfilled only with the coming of Jesus. How do you respond to the idea of remaining faithful for your whole life, waiting for something that won't be fulfilled until after you're dead? Can you have faith like that? Why or why not?

8 What is your personal takeaway from these passages from Matthew and Hebrews?

Journal Time

Below is a series of words that describe positive or neutral personality traits. Circle *three to five* of these that you think are true of you. Then journal about them, describing how they play out in your life and how they equip you to contribute to good in the world.

inventive
love art
cooperative
love reading
energetic
self-disciplined
sociable
compassionate
helpful
not easily fooled
stable
reasonable
bold
warm
thorough
versatile
cautious
flexible
analytical
kind

curious
passionate
imaginative
practical
assertive
good planner
reflective
good with computers
well-tempered
confident
dynamic
enthusiastic
expressive
tactful
industrious
diplomatic
independent
thoughtful
moderate
dependable

consistent
adventurous
systematic
good with data
perceptive
spontaneous
outgoing
friendly
trustworthy
secure
adaptable
communicative
sympathetic
firm
tireless
deep
intellectual
organized
persistent
patient

Listening

PRAYER ACTIVITY

Write a letter to God telling him *one* of the following:

- The things about your personality and character that make you unsure whether you fit in with God's people or have the potential to serve God powerfully.
- The things about your personality and character that people in your childhood or adulthood made fun of or said were negatives.

List the things here to reference in your letter.

Now write God's response. If you'd like, write out Romans 8:31–39 or Ephesians 2:1–10.

RAHAB SESSION 4

You Have a Choice

Memory Verse

"Before I formed you in the womb I knew you,
before you were born I set you apart."

(Jeremiah 1:5 NIV)

Select a volunteer
to read the following:

As women, many of us spend a lot of time listing all the reasons why we're not qualified. We're not good at something. There's something wrong with us. We can't succeed. We're damaged goods. We'll fail, so why try? But through the life of Rahab, we see the only bullet point that matters: *In Christ, we are qualified.* Through his death, we can kill off every lie on that list. Through his resurrection, we can give life to new thoughts and behaviors. Rahab was a damaged prostitute. She was considered an unimportant person where she came from. She was raised in a corrupt, anti-God culture—a culture so bad that God intended to wipe it off the map. Yet none of that disqualified her from doing something great for God's plan. She didn't let the fear of failure stop her from trying. She didn't let the judgment her culture deserved stop her from reaching out and asking for deliverance from that judgment. She went from judged to qualified because of one thing: She chose to believe in the real God and who he said she was.

In this final session on Rahab, we'll see that this God knows exactly what it's like to be us because he has walked this earth in our shoes. We'll see that he covers our shame and protects our vulnerable parts. And we'll see that he has made us fully qualified to participate in what he is doing in the world. We have everything we need. All we need to do is trust and respond.

Check In

Before you dive into the video, take a few minutes to check in with each other. Let each person choose one of the following questions to respond to:

- What did you get out of the "On Your Own" activities you did for Session 3?
- Where did you see God at work in your life this week? Or where did you hope to see him and didn't?

Next, say your memory verse aloud together, along with its reference.

At a Glance RAHAB

Age-old problem: Having flaws and weaknesses

Age-old mistake: Disqualifying ourselves from God's service

God's timeless wisdom: God makes us qualified. He uses everything we have been for his mission: *"For we are God's masterpiece. He has created us anew in Christ Jesus, so we can do the good things he planned for us long ago" (Ephesians 2:10 NLT).*

Video Notes

Play the video segment for Session 4. It's about 20 minutes long. As you watch, use the following outline to record thoughts that stand out to you.

DRAMA: Nicole

Jesus didn't come to save us from our circumstances. He came to find us in the midst of them, so that we could know he knows right where we're walking.

When God knocks, we open the door and the journey, as hard as it is, will never be wasted.

TEACHING: Jada

One of the most dangerous things women do to themselves is disqualification.

Everyone has had opportunities to respond to God.

Is your background or personality diminishing your hope?

Even if things don't change overnight, we can trust God that he is working them out. Hope is going to come to fruition.

TEACHING: *Kasey*

Before Rahab was in the womb, God knew her and formed her for purpose and meaning.

The curse on Noah's son Ham: Genesis 9:18–27.

Prophecy is a message that aligns with the already finished will of God.

Hesed ("kindness" in Joshua 2:12–14 NIV) means a love that covers, protects, keeps safe.

God does not point out our shame, vulnerabilities, and weaknesses. Instead, he covers them.

God is going to restore all that has been exposed, all that has been violated.

Group Discussion

Leader, read each numbered prompt to the group.

1 What stood out to you most from the video?

2 How does it affect you to think of God having walked in your shoes and wasting nothing you have been through?

3 Jada said, "I think that one of the most dangerous things that women do to themselves is disqualification." What does it mean to disqualify yourself? How do we as women do it?

How is disqualification a choice?

4 Rahab had *"the assurance of things hoped for" (Hebrews 11:1 ESV).* What do you hope for? How much assurance do you have that you will one day get it?

5 How do we know if we are hoping for the right things?

6 Could your past or your personality be diminishing your hope? If so, how?

7 Why did Rahab need a love that covers, protects, and keeps safe?

Why do we need that same kind of love?

8 Why is it important that God doesn't point out our shame but instead covers it? How can that affect the way we feel and live?

9 When you think of God restoring all that has been exposed and violated, what do you think that will look like and feel like?

10 You answered the following question at the beginning of Session 1 (p. 14). Take a minute on your own and write down how you would respond to it now: How much do you believe God can work through you to accomplish his plan for good in the world? A lot? A little? What helps you believe that? What gets in the way?

11 Discuss this with your group: What are you grateful for that you've received from this study on Rahab? What will you take with you?

Select a volunteer

to read the following:

Hope is longing for something you don't yet have. The more you want it, the more you ache: *"Hope deferred makes the heart sick" (Proverbs 13:12 NIV).* Because many of us have had our hopes disappointed and betrayed way too often, we have tried to deaden the ache of hope in our hearts. But deadening hope also deadens other things in our hearts, like the capacity for joy and generous love. We become tough. Things don't get to us. And people don't get through to the real us either. When that happens, coming back alive to hope and love takes time and commitment. We have to be willing to feel the sadness of our losses and disappointments. And we need a vision of what God offers us that we can hope for with confidence. We have a choice to make.

In preparation for the coming week, write one thing you want to gain from your study time:

(ex.: hope for my future, a better understanding of who I am . . .)

Closing Prayer

Ask for a volunteer to read this prayer aloud over the group:

God, thank you for your love that covers our vulnerabilities and shame, that protects, that keeps safe. Thank you for revealing yourself to us and inviting us to respond to you. Thank you for walking in our shoes and knowing, really knowing, what it is like to be us. Please help us not to disqualify ourselves, but instead, actively engage our story—looking for ways to renew our past, not run from it. Please help us to respond to you with hope, with faith, like Rahab. We give to you all of our doubts that you can work through us to accomplish your good plan, and we trust that you can use us with all of our complicated history and personality. Please show us our next step. We pray in Jesus' name, amen.

Keep This Close

As you go on your way this week, here are some thoughts from the video that you may want to save in your phone or write on a sticky note so you can refer back to them:

- I don't have to be stuck. I can be used by the sovereign God.
- God is going to restore all that has been exposed, all that has been violated.

RAHAB
SESSION 4

On Your Own

Memory Verse

"Before I formed you in the womb I knew you,
before you were born I set you apart."

(Jeremiah 1:5 NIV)

In Real Life:

DRAMA ACTIVITY: Shoes, Part 2

Nicole took us back to the story of the shoes she wore as a child and teen, and she realized that God had gone to find her right in the middle of agonizing circumstances. He has wasted nothing she has been through.

1 How well do the shoes that Jesus has given you fit your feet? Do you still need Band-Aids or cushions? Why?

2 What does walking in the shoes designed just for you feel like?

3 Do you still want to wear someone else's shoes, or are you able to value your own? Describe what you value about yours or whose shoes you would rather wear.

4 When Peter had doubts about whether non-Jews could become fully qualified followers of Jesus, God gave him a vision. In the vision God said, *"Do not call something unclean if God has made it clean" (Acts 11:9 NLT).* How do these words apply to you today?

5 Paul worked for the arrest and murder of Christians before he had a vision of Jesus and changed his views. He then went on to use everything he had learned as a Jewish student and all of his experience as a forgiven man with blood on his hands to form the message he shared with people about Jesus. Read 1 Timothy 1:12–17. Can you identify with Paul calling himself the foremost sinner (verse 15), or does that seem foreign to you? Why?

According to Paul, why did he receive mercy (verse 16)?

Does this help to explain to you why you have received mercy? Explain.

6 Read Psalm 139:14. Can you authentically say, "I am wonderfully made"? What helps you? What gets in the way?

Rahab in The Bible

SCRIPTURE ACTIVITY

Look up James 2:14–26 and read it.

In Hebrews 11, the writer points to Rahab as an example of faith. James, the brother of Jesus, also writes about Rahab and faith. They both agree that faith isn't simply agreeing with information about God. Rahab chose to believe she was worth God noticing her—she was qualified to be loved because He said she was. And then she acted on that conviction.

1 What is the true connection between conviction and action (verse 22)?

2 How did Rahab express her conviction in action (verse 25)?

3 Do you believe you are qualified to be loved because God says you are? As this study draws to a close, what encourages you to believe this? Does anything still get in the way?

4 How could you express in action your conviction about being qualified?

5 What is your personal takeaway from thinking about the connection between conviction and action? How would you say it if you were going to post it online?

Journal Time

Choose *one* of the following topics to journal about:

- Romans 1:20 means that everybody has had opportunities to respond to God. What opportunities have you had? How have you responded to those opportunities? Which ones have you made excuses about or disqualified yourself for? Which ones have you responded to with faith and action? What do you want to do now?
- Do you have a habit of disqualifying yourself? If so, how does that tend to play out? Where do you think the habit comes from?
- Think about God restoring all that has been exposed and violated in you. Let yourself imagine that this is in the process of happening. How will you be different? How will that change the choices that have become automatic in you?
- *Hesed* is a love that covers, protects, and keeps safe. Why do you need that kind of love? How will it affect your life if you get it?

Whichever topic you choose, finish up by writing about this question:

- What will you do differently in your day-to-day life as a result of this study?

Take Action

What would it look like for you to put faith like Rahab's into action? To what deeds is God calling you? Spend some time in prayer about this. Look around you at the needs of people in your world. Consider your personality, your skills, and your other resources. In *Wishful Thinking*, author Frederick Buechner says, "The place God calls you to is the place where your deep gladness and the world's deep hunger meet." Write down your thoughts about steps you can take to contribute to what God is doing in the world.

Welcome to Week 5

HAGAR

In the Face of Rejection, God Says I'm *Significant*

Emotion IN THE **MOMENT** CAN MAKE US **FORGET** THE CONSEQUENCE OF OUR DECISION.

HAGAR
SESSION 5

Exposing the Lie of Shame

Memory Verse

She gave this name to the LORD who spoke to her: "You are the God who sees me."

(GENESIS 16:13 NIV)

Select a volunteer
to read the following:

Many of us are on a never-ending quest to counter messages from our world that we are insignificant. Maybe the message of insignificance comes from comparing ourselves to those who have wealth and status, or maybe we compare our perception of beauty. Maybe our idea of insignificance stems from stories of "better" mothers, or others who seem to have a sense of purpose that we lack. We may put enormous effort into a social media presence that says we have life all together and are achieving what we "should" be achieving. Yet in one instant, social media can shatter our security and make us question, "Do I measure up? Should I be doing this the way *she* does?"

In this study we'll be introduced to a woman of the Bible named Hagar, the slave of an insecure and impatient woman named Sarah. (We all have some Sarah in us.) We'll see how both Hagar and Sarah were desperate for significance, mired in the feeling that the world saw them as deficient, and hiding their shame by mistreating others. We'll also discover that we're not doomed to be stuck in patterns like this, because God sees us, he knows us, and he can be the person we run to when the world tells us we don't matter.

Check In

Welcome to the first session of Hagar: In the Face of Rejection, God Says I'm Significant. To get started, give everyone a chance to do the following:

- Take one minute to tell a little about what your life was like in junior high school.
- Take a minute on your own and write down your response to this question (you won't have to share your answer): On a scale of 0 to 5, how confident are you that you totally belong to God despite your popularity or platform in the world? Mark where you are on the continuum below.

0	1	2	3	4	5
Not at all confident					Very confident

Video Notes

Play the video segment for Session 5. It's about 20 minutes long. As you watch, use the following outline to record thoughts that stand out to you.

DRAMA: *Nicole*

Feeling insignificant can lead to feeling like you don't matter.

Being treated like you are insignificant can lead to feeling like you are invisible.

At a Glance: HAGAR

Age-old problem: Shame over feeling deficient in some way

Age-old mistake: Trying to hide shame by treating someone else like she's deficient

God's timeless wisdom: Run to God for refuge and acceptance: *But I am not ashamed, for I know whom I have believed, and I am convinced that he is able to guard until that day what has been entrusted to me (2 Timothy 1:12 ESV).* It is difficult to feel less than or deficient when you first consider Jesus. Think of him first and your whole perspective of self will be righted; the shame the world may be throwing at you will suddenly seem irrational and irrelevant. Jesus stands guard on our behalf and defends our worth.

TEACHING: *Jada*

Sometimes we are a victim of someone else's choices (parents' addiction, bad relationships, etc.).

Sometimes the emotion of the moment can make us forget the consequences of our decisions.

You can love Jesus and still feel like your life is heading in the wrong direction.

TEACHING: *Kasey*

Shame is a feeling that starts with embarrassment, can quickly move to anger, and then to pride.

Shame will always look like hiding.

Remember the question: Does this reinforce or does this release my shame?

Group Discussion

Leader, read each numbered prompt to the group.

1 What stood out to you most from the video?

2 Hagar was in part a victim of Sarah's and Abraham's choices. *They* chose to stop waiting for God to give them a child. *They* chose to make Hagar the surrogate mother for a child Abraham would have with her, a child they would adopt as their legal heir. She didn't have a say in the matter. What are some ways we today can be victims of someone else's choices?

3 What do you think we can do about being victims of someone else's choices? What can God do?

4 Jada talked about hope. How strong are you in hope right now? What motivates you to have hope? What gets in the way?

5 How do you define shame? What can move us to feel shame today?

6 What does hiding from shame look like in our behavior today? Give some examples. Think of examples that involve attacking others as well as examples that look meek.

7 Read Hebrews 6:17–20. Instead of hiding in shame, we can flee for refuge to God's inner sanctuary, where Jesus has gone before us. How do you think fleeing for refuge in God is different from hiding in shame behind church or Bible study or spiritual practices?

GOD'S not just your **hope,** he's your *purpose.*

Select a volunteer
to read the following:

Shame always leads to hiding in some way. For example, Sarah felt shame over being unable to bear a child. In her culture, bearing children was the number one way women proved their worth to society. Without children, women were often seen as useless. Sarah decided she would hide behind her servant Hagar. Hagar would have a child with Abraham, and society would count it as Sarah's.

Unfortunately for Sarah, Hagar felt shame too. So, when Hagar got pregnant, she decided to hide her shame by tossing words, facial expressions, and body language of contempt at Sarah. Shame and hiding don't always move a person to become a wilting wallflower; they often move a person to lash out at others.

In preparation for the coming week, write one thing you want to gain from your study time:

(ex: hope for my future, a better understanding of who I am . . .)

Closing Prayer

Ask for a volunteer to read this prayer aloud over the group:

Creator God, thank you that you can bring good out of our suffering when we have been the victims of other people's choices. Thank you that you can even bring good out of our suffering when we have made choices that have landed us in places of forced servitude. We put into your hands all our shame and all of the ways we hide from you and other people. Please come to us in our places of hiding and lead us out. We want to choose to take refuge in you. Thank you that you fully accept us as we are, in all our messiness. In Jesus' name, amen.

Keep This Close

As you go on your way this week, here are some thoughts from the video that you may want to save in your phone or write on a sticky note so you can refer back to them:

- Even when we feel like victims, in God we are vindicated.
- God fully accepts us. He has set us free from condemnation and shame.
- Instead of hiding from people, we can run to God for refuge.

HAGAR
SESSION 5

On Your Own

Memory Verse

She gave this name to the Lord *who spoke to her:*
"You are the God who sees me."

(Genesis 16:13 niv)

New Memory Verse This Week! In this verse, Hagar is coming to multiple conclusions about her past, her present, and ultimately her future. She claims or names God *El Roi*, which means "God sees me." Think about that for a moment. In an instant, Hagar is made aware that she is not only seen, but her life matters and is recognized. Her pain, struggle, insecurity—vindicated at once because God declares that he sees her, he is paying attention, he has her.

In Real Life:

DRAMA ACTIVITY: Enough, Part 1

A former waitress becomes the manager of the diner where she works. She accepts the position because she needs the extra money to support herself and her young daughter. But the job begins to take over her life so that she scarcely sees her daughter anymore. This would be hard enough, but she feels the owners misled her and now treat her as if she doesn't matter.

1. Do you think the character in the story was correct in her assessment of her situation? What informs your belief?

2 What features of your life (if any) send you the message that you don't matter?

3 Are there roles or responsibilities in your life that tell you that you do matter? What are those things? Are there people to whom you matter who let you know this?

4 How would getting the message that you don't matter affect your behavior? For example, if you got that message, what might you do to compensate or to make yourself feel better? How might you try to protect yourself from people? Or how could you hide from them?

5 Read 1 Peter 2:9–10. The apostle Peter wrote to some scattered groups of people from a variety of ethnic backgrounds. He wrote to them about being a chosen race and a royal priesthood. Do you believe deep down that you are part of a group that God has set apart? Would it change anything if you believed this? What would change?

6 What might it take for you to be convinced that God has chosen you?

7 When God picked Abraham to be the head of a chosen family, he didn't do it in order to form an exclusive club for people who could feel like they were better than everybody else. He did it to show Abraham's family what it was like to be blessed *in order that they could then be a blessing* to all the families of the world (Genesis 12:3). Likewise, today when God chooses people from all over the world to be part of his family, he doesn't do it for them to feel like they are better than those around them. He does it to make them a blessing to the world. How does this affect the way you view the idea of being chosen?

Hagar in the Bible

SCRIPTURE ACTIVITY

Look up Genesis 16:1–6 and read it.

God had a long-range plan to rescue human beings from the consequences of their attempts to run their own lives apart from him. He planned to rescue all families by first focusing on one family. That family was going to be the descendants of a Middle Eastern man named Abraham. God had promised Abraham that all the families of the earth would be blessed through him. There was just one problem: Abraham and his wife, Sarah, kept getting older and older, and Sarah never got pregnant.

Our story picks up when Sarah was far past menopause. (At this point, Sarah is called Sarai and Abraham is called Abram. God would change their names later.)

1 In the group discussion, you talked about how Hagar was the victim of other people's choices. On the other hand, what choices did she make herself in verse 4? In verse 6?

2 What do these choices reflect about Hagar?

3 Shame is a feeling of being seen and found deficient. Sarah felt deficient because she was childless. Hagar felt deficient too. Have you ever felt deficient in some way? Do you still feel deficient in any area? If so, why?

4 Shame leads to the desire to hide and not be seen. There are a number of common hiding behaviors. When we hide, we may treat other people with contempt, as if they are worthless or deserve scorn. Or we may treat ourselves with contempt. Would you say Sarah is more inclined to treat herself or other people with contempt? How does she show that? How does Hagar show contempt?

5 What about you? Have you ever treated someone else with contempt, even subtly? If so, what did that look like in your actions or words? Have you ever treated yourself with contempt? If so, what did that look like?

6 What are a couple of posts that Hagar might have made over the course of her pregnancy?

7 What is your takeaway from this study? What do you want to do about it?

Shame and Hiding

CONNECTION ACTIVITY

Shame leads to hiding. We can hide behind:

- Our husband, children, or another relationship
- Our status—being considered influential, smart, honorable, respectable, successful, or spiritual
- A job
- Popularity or approval by a certain group
- Our looks or our smile
- Bible knowledge, church volunteering
- Busyness
- Social media

Use your answers to these questions to journal on your own and process through your prayer time.

1. Are you hiding? If so, what are you hiding behind? That is, what do you use to distract people from looking directly at you as you really are?

2. When do you hide? Are there certain people or situations you hide from, or do you hide from everybody all the time?

3. Think of your behaviors and relationships. Which ones reinforce your shame? Which ones make you more aware of your inadequacies? Which ones lead to feelings of condemnation?

4 Think of your behaviors and relationships again. Which ones restore confidence and help to release your shame? Which ones draw you closer, especially on your bad days? Which ones lead you to the truth? Which ones cause in you a longing to change? Which ones convict you without condemning you?

5 What do you want to do differently in your day-to-day life as a result of this reflection?

As a believer, we get to **HIDE.** We just have to **HIDE** in the *right place.*

Journal Time

Choose *one* of the following topics to journal about:

- Have you ever been the victim of someone else's choices? If so, what was that person's choice? How did it affect you? (For instance, how did it hurt you, cause you shame, help you grow, isolate you, cause you anxiety or fear or some other emotion, or increase your understanding of something?) How did you respond (or how are you responding)? What results came from your response? What do you think would be the best available response to that situation?
- Are you currently in a situation that makes you question if God knows what he's doing? If so, what's going on that prompts that thought? What feelings are you having about your situation? (Get them all out in an uncensored way. Use colored pens if that inspires you.) How did you get here? How have you been trying to manage your feelings and the situation? How is that working? What do you think would be the best way to respond to your situation?
- Have you been mistreated by anyone in authority over you? If so, what happened? What feelings have you had about that? How have you responded in actions and attitudes? What have been the results? Colossians 3:23 says, *"Whatever you do, work heartily, as for the Lord and not for men" (ESV).* If God is your purpose, not success or achievement or fairness, you will be better equipped to deal with mistreatment. How helpful is it for you to think about that? Why? What do you think God wants us to do if we have been abused or if someone at work has crossed the line of harassment?

Whichever topic you choose, finish by answering this question:

- What do I want to do differently in my day-to-day life as a result of this reflection?

Listening

PRAYER ACTIVITY

In our insanely busy world, it's enormously valuable to set aside even a few minutes away from the distractions of life to think about what God might be trying to get through to you. God speaks to the heart—the core of you, where your thoughts, emotions, desires, motives, and choices come from. He speaks above all through the Bible. He also speaks in other ways, such as through his people. He can speak through circumstances, using them to highlight something he has said in his Word. He doesn't give "new revelation" that contradicts what has been written, but he does guide you in how his words apply to your unique life. Sometimes he is trying to get through to us about a blind spot that others see or about a hard decision we are facing, but we can't hear him over the noise in our lives.

Find a quiet place where you can be alone. Maybe take a walk, sit on the porch, head to the nearest park bench, or simply sit in your car alone for a few minutes. Turn off your phone—or better still, leave it somewhere else so it doesn't draw your eye and your thoughts. Lay before God whatever you have read or heard recently from the Bible. Lay before him any shame you have and any tendency to hide. Offer him your worries. Think of at least three things you have to be thankful for and thank him for those. If there are things people have said to you, or said in your group meeting, that stick in your mind, ask God what he might be saying to you through those. Invite him to put together the pieces of what you need to hear from him. Then see if you can rest in the silence for a few minutes. If you get distracted, gently turn your mind back to your memory verse or one of the things you're thankful for. Don't be discouraged if you don't hear an audible message from God. Just being more open to him is the important thing.

HAGAR
SESSION 6

Rejected to Accepted

Memory Verse

She gave this name to the L*ORD who spoke to her:*
"You are the God who sees me."

(Genesis 16:13 NIV)

Select a volunteer
to read the following:

Hagar was a slave. When Sarah told her to have a child with Abraham, she didn't have the freedom to say no. When she ran away from Sarah, she had nowhere to go if she didn't want to die in the desert. Compared to her, we may have lots of options to say no or go somewhere new and start over.

But despite our external freedoms, we may still experience internal bondage—we may be held captive to a painful memory, unresolved relationship, or unhealthy habit. Regardless of the presentation, all captivity comes from the same place: the fear of being rejected upon exposure.

What can we do about this fear? In this study, we'll see what Hagar did. We'll discover that transformation starts when we come to believe God's promise that he knows and accepts us fully, even on our worst days. And we'll explore ways of coming to believe this deep down where it counts. We don't have to be in bondage to anything—even fear. God wants to set us free.

Check In

Before you dive into the video, take a few minutes to check in with each other. Let each person choose one of the following questions to respond to:

- What did you get out of the "On Your Own" activities you did for Session 5?
- When you were a child, what did people around you do when you misbehaved?

Next, say your memory verse for this study on Hagar aloud together. Be sure to say the verse reference after it. If you don't know the verse from memory yet, read it with the group from page 125.

- Try to recite your memory verse from your study of Rahab aloud together as a group. (hint: Jeremiah 1:5)

At a Glance: HAGAR

Age-old problem: Harsh treatment

Age-old mistake: Run away

God's timeless wisdom: Trust that God sees. He sees what you are going through and he is with you. Stay and work for what is right when possible; you are not alone. Running does not get you further from God, it only delays your reunion: *"'You are the God who sees me,' for she said, 'I have now seen the One who sees me'" (Genesis 16:13 NIV).*

Video Notes

Play the video segment for Session 6. It's about 20 minutes long. As you watch, use the following outline to record thoughts that stand out to you.

DRAMA: Nicole

Running doesn't resolve what's unresolved inside of us.

TEACHING: Kasey

Freedom is any place in us that believes we are fully and finally accepted in God.

God doesn't want us to make peace with our bondage.

What is wrong? Where in my heart have I gone to get to this place as a Christian?

At the root of our slavery is the fear of rejection.

Satan loves when we withdraw from people.

We can get **stuck** looking at the "WHAT." But *freedom* is **found** in the "WHY."

Group Discussion

Leader, read each numbered prompt to the group.

1 What stood out to you most from the video?

2 The drama was about a woman knitting and talking about running away. Do you tend to run away from people and problems? Or do you stay and face them? Give an example.

3 Kasey said, "Freedom is any place in us that believes we are fully and finally accepted in God." What are some of the behaviors of someone who truly believes she is fully accepted by God, even on her worst days?

4 What are some of the behaviors of a person who isn't sure she is fully and finally accepted by God? Try to think of a wide variety of behaviors that might reflect this doubt.

5 Describe ways you can recognize when someone accepts you as a person.

6 How does the fear of rejection sabotage meaningful relationships? Think about the behaviors that might flow from a fear of rejection. Then think about how those behaviors affect relationships. List some here.

7 Satan can harass us when we withdraw from others. What does withdrawing look like? Try to think of as many different ways of withdrawing as you can. For instance, how can we withdraw while still being around people? List the ways you withdraw here.

8 When we start thinking in extreme ways, we think in terms of "always" and "never." "I will never be enough. I will always be misunderstood. I can never go back to that church. I will always be alone. I must end this relationship completely because there is no hope of reconciliation." Together, fill in the blanks with other "always" and "never" statements that we might believe.

I will always ______________________________.

I will never ______________________________.

He will always ______________________________.

He will never ______________________________.

Select a volunteer

to read the following:

God accepts a *person* without approving of all of her *behavior*. God grieves and disciplines all behavior that draws us away from his goodness. He loves and forgives us even on our worst days and in our most destructive behaviors. He demonstrated that when Jesus was arrested and tortured and sent to the cross. As he was dying in that horrific manner, Jesus said of the very people who had crucified him, *"Father, forgive them, for they know not what they do" (Luke 23:34 ESV).*

This can be hard for us to believe if we have had the experience of being rejected because of our behavior. We all have bad days, as children or adults, and people haven't always treated us with love and forgiveness on those days. But we can learn that God is different and that some people are different as well.

In preparation for the coming week, write one thing you want to gain from your study time:

(ex: hope for my future, a better understanding of who I am . . .)

Closing Prayer

Ask a volunteer to read this prayer aloud over the group:

Father God, in the midst of his suffering, your Son forgave his persecutors for what they did to him. Please help us believe that you accept us on our worst days with our worst behavior. Please help us believe what you say about us in the Bible. Go into the scared, unfree parts of us, and speak your words of acceptance and healing to those places. Thank you for the other women in this group. Let your Holy Spirit go with them as they walk through this week, and keep speaking words of acceptance to them. In Jesus' name, amen.

Keep This Close

As you go on your way this week, here are some thoughts from the video that you may want to save in your phone or write on a sticky note so you can refer back to them:

- Freedom is any place in us that believes we are fully and finally accepted in God.
- *"He has sent me to proclaim liberty to the captives, and recovering of sight to the blind" (Luke 4:18 ESV).*

HAGAR
SESSION 6

On Your Own

Memory Verse

She gave this name to the LORD who spoke to her:
"You are the God who sees me."

(GENESIS 16:13 NIV)

In Real Life:

DRAMA ACTIVITY: Cut and Run

In the drama, a woman reflected on her life while knitting. Looking back, she realized that she was a person who simply cut the yarn when things got tangled up. In other words, she ran away. She has come to see the value in a long skein of yarn.

1 How would you describe your life in terms of knitting? For instance, is your life like one big ball of yarn that can be used for a whole project? Is it cut up into pieces? Is it a tangled mess, or have you worked to untangle portions of it?

2 Have you ever run away from someone or something? What have been the consequences of your running away, or not running away?

3 If God were to knit your life into one harmonious whole, what are some of the pieces you would like him to draw together?

4 Read Luke 15:11–32. This is Jesus' great story about a young man who runs away. Or is it? In truth, both young men run away from their father in different ways. How does each son run away from his father?

5 What does the father do about each son's choice to run away from him?

6 The younger son eventually decides to go home. What does the father's response to him say about the father?

7 We aren't told whether the older son ever decides to truly go home to his father. How does this affect what you take away from the story?

8 Which son are you more like? How? What would going home to the father look like in your life today?

Hagar in the Bible

SCRIPTURE ACTIVITY

Look up Genesis 16:7–16 and reread this part of Hagar's story.

When we last saw Hagar, she was running away from Sarah after Sarah abused her. Hagar is pregnant. She is Egyptian, so naturally she flees in the direction of Egypt. But between her and Egypt is the vast Sinai desert. She gets as far as a spring many days into the desert when the angel of the Lord speaks to her.

1. If you were alone and pregnant in the middle of a desert, who could you call? What would you post on social media?

2. In verse 8, the angel asks Hagar a question, and she doesn't fully answer it. She says where she has come from, but she doesn't say where she is going. That says a lot about her situation. Consider what the angel says in verse 9. How do you think the angel's words affect Hagar? Why?

3 Would you be encouraged by the angel's words in verses 10-12? Why or why not?

4 God's instruction to Hagar may seem harsh, but she was in a situation with no good options. She was a pregnant woman in the desert, vulnerable to heat, hunger, thirst, wild animals, and abuse by nomadic traders. Going back to Abraham and Sarah may have been her only choice for survival. Think about how Hagar responds to the angel's words in verse 13. What do her words say about how the angel's words have affected her?

5 Why do you think she feels that God has seen her?

6 Do you feel that God has seen you? Why or why not?

7 God doesn't make new circumstances possible for Hagar at this point. She has to go back to Abraham and Sarah. How does that make you feel about God? Why?

Fear of rejection allows men to have the power only GOD should.

Journal Time

Choose *one* of the following topics to journal about:

- Are you finally and fully accepted in Jesus? Do you truly believe him when he says you are? What in your life suggests that you do believe him? What in your life suggests that you don't? What helps you believe him? What gets in the way? Who could help you get past the events you have experienced that tell you there are things you have to do to earn acceptance?
- What are the things you have done or are doing that make you wonder whether you have disqualified yourself from God's full acceptance? Give some thought to your past, and identify those things that make you think, "Nope, God can't accept me with that." Then give some focused thought to your actions and habits now, and see if there is anything that makes you think, *No, it is too much for God to love me while I'm doing that.*
- Reflect on one of the destructive things you have done. Let God ask you, "What's wrong?" Let him ask you gently and lovingly, "Why did you do that?" Where in your heart had you gone to get to the place where you did that?
- What are some of the things you have done, or that you do now, to try to earn love from God or another person? What have been the consequences of those actions? How do they affect you? How do they affect other people? How do they affect the way you relate to God?
- What are you scared of? Are you scared of your honest story? Of being vulnerable? Of stepping out into something new and unknown? Of just being a regular woman? Are you scared of the rejection that might happen to you if you take action?

Whichever topic you choose, finish up by answering this question:

- What will I choose to do differently in my day-to-day life as a result of this reflection? Use extra paper if necessary.

Memories of Rejection

CONNECTION ACTIVITY

We can push memories of rejection deep into our subconscious and never deal with them. Over time, they fracture us, inside and outside. They can keep us from having really meaningful relationships.

Think back over your past from your earliest memories, through your time at school, until now. When did you experience rejection? When were you not fully accepted on your worst days? When did you think you needed to earn someone's love?

Choose *one* of those memories, and using the space provided, describe:

- The person or people who didn't accept you
- What they did to send a rejecting message
- Where you were
- Anyone else who was involved or looking on
- How this affected your life: your growth; your hurt; your isolation; your feelings of anxiety, fear, shame, anger, numbness; your understanding of yourself; your understanding of God
- What is your part now? Where do you need to take ownership, make amends, reach out, forgive?
- How can you use this part of your past to glorify God and do good to others in the future?

Listening

PRAYER ACTIVITY

Do you have trouble embracing the truth that God accepts you even on your worst days? If so, take some time to pray over Romans 8:33–34 below:

Who will bring any charge against those whom God has chosen? It is God who justifies. Who then is the one who condemns? No one. Christ Jesus who died—more than that, who was raised to life—is at the right hand of God and is also interceding for us. (NIV)

Give yourself at least ten minutes to write a prayer about this passage. Talk with God about how you know he has chosen you, or why you're not sure. Tell him about any people from your present or your past whose voices bringing charges against you seem to frequently resonate in your head. Where are those voices of condemnation coming from? What do you think Jesus says about them? Ask him to show you why it matters that he died and was raised to life. Thank Jesus that he is interceding for you. Ask God to help you truly believe that he accepts you. Pour out your thoughts and feelings to him, the whole story that maybe you normally hold back because you're not sure if he can deal with it.

HAGAR
SESSION 7

Trusting After Betrayal

Memory Verse

She gave this name to the Lord who spoke to her:
"You are the God who sees me."

(Genesis 16:13 niv)

Select a volunteer
to read the following:

Hagar was exploited by people in authority, people who were followers of God. This happens with tragic frequency. It may have even happened to you. Authority figures, churchgoers, and even church leaders are imperfect and sometimes shockingly selfish. When they fail to treat others with love and respect, those who are mistreated often conclude that the people of God can't be trusted. Some, indeed, cannot be. But if we make this a blanket statement about all of God's people, it is easy to cut ourselves off from the healing partnership God promises through a faith community. In fact, the more distance we put between ourselves and those empowered by the Holy Spirit, the less we experience and acknowledge God's work. We may even be distanced from God as we distance ourselves from God's people.

If this describes you, if you have been hiding out at the margins of a church community because you've been burned, or if you have been avoiding church altogether, don't give up. Hagar shows us that an awful situation like this can be redeemed. Whether you have been harmed by people in the church or out of the church, God can restore you to a place where you can feel safe being in partnership with people again. In this study we will consider how healing happens, how to build a healthy church community, and what forgiveness is and isn't. You aren't stuck with your hurts. God can bring good to a tragic story in ways that you may never have expected.

Check In

Before you dive into the video, take a few minutes to check in with each other. Give everyone a chance to respond to one of the following questions:

- → What did you get out of the "On Your Own" activities you did for Session 6?
- → When someone wrongs you or hurts you, how do you typically respond? (You can choose more than one answer or come up with your own.)

____ I express anger at them.
____ I hold a grudge.
____ I withdraw.
____ I let it go.
____ Other (name it):

Next, say your memory verse aloud together. Be sure to say the verse reference with it. Give it a try to recite Jeremiah 1:5 together as a group also!

At a Glance: HAGAR

Age-old problem: Betrayal by followers of God

Age-old mistake: Distancing yourself from other people and refusing to trust

God's timeless wisdom: Put your trust in God, and learn from him to treat other people with love even if they're not trustworthy: *"O my God, in you I trust; let me not be put to shame; let not my enemies exult over me"* (Psalm 25:2 ESV); *"But love your enemies, and do good, and lend, expecting nothing in return, and your reward will be great, and you will be sons of the Most High, for he is kind to the ungrateful and the evil. Be merciful, even as your Father is merciful"* (Luke 6:35–36 ESV).

Video Notes

Play the video segment for Session 7. It's about 18 minutes long. As you watch, use the following outline to record thoughts that stand out to you.

DRAMA: Nicole

God can't always get you out, but he will sit right with you.

You're right where you're supposed to be. And you're not alone. God is right here with you. And that's better than out.

TEACHING: Jada

Some people have trust issues because they have been hurt by people in authority, including in the church.

You were created in the image of God, regardless of how anyone has treated you.

A huge part of trusting God is understanding what's hurting your heart, doing the hard work, and making the choice to let it go.

You can't be used greatly by God when all of your energy is hugging tightly the things that have hurt you.

Find the community you need to be in so you can find healing.

Being hurt by **God's people** isn't the same as being hurt by GOD.

Group Discussion

Leader, read each numbered prompt to the group.

1 What stood out to you most from the video?

2 Jada talked about how many people she has known who have been hurt by those in authority, especially in the church. What do you think it is about churches that makes this scenario all too common?

3 Jada says, however, that the solution is not for us to avoid churches. What's wrong with this as a solution? What do we lose when we avoid churches, or when we just duck in, attend the service, and then duck out again without getting involved?

4 What can we do to make church a safe and healthy place for people to get involved? How can we contribute?

5 How do you think a person can heal after she has suffered a violation of her trust? What does she need to do? What help does she need from people? What help does she need from God?

6 God asks us to forgive those who have harmed us. Why do you suppose this is often so hard for us to do?

7 How does knowing that you were created in God's image—and that you are his—help you deal with the ways you have been hurt?

Select a volunteer
to read the following:

Jada talked about the importance of understanding what is hurting our hearts. Burying the hurt won't help us truly move on. Rehearsing our resentment over and over won't help us move on either. We need to come to understand what happened to us, why it hurts so much, and how it is still affecting us. We may need the help of a wise and trusted person, or several people, to gain this kind of understanding. It is sometimes hard to come to understand our own pain without talking about it with someone who will listen, not judge, and help us explore how it is affecting who we are now.

Jada also spoke of forgiveness, which lets go of the desire to get even or get what is fair. Forgiveness does not mean saying what the other person did to us was okay, and it doesn't mean saying the pain is insignificant. Forgiveness simply means choosing to let go of the bitterness and the desire to make others pay for what they did.

In preparation for the coming week, write one thing you want to gain from your study time:

(ex: hope for my future, a better understanding of who I am . . .)

Closing Prayer

Ask a volunteer to read this prayer aloud over the group:

God of heaven and earth, you are the one in charge of justice, of allowing people to face the consequences of their wrong actions. We want to let go of the hurt that has come from the people who have harmed us. Help us lay down our desire to see that they "get what they deserve," knowing that there have been times by your grace that we have not had to suffer what we deserve. We offer these hurts to you, these people to you, and we ask your help in truly entrusting them to *your* justice, believing you will help our feelings catch up to our choice. We also ask you to heal our broken ability to trust and enable us to enter into relationships going forward where we can be honest, vulnerable, and safe. Thank you that you are with us. You have climbed into the backseat to comfort us in our pain and you will never leave us. We are yours, always and forever. In Jesus' name, amen.

Keep This Close

As you go on your way this week, here are some thoughts from the video that you may want to save in your phone or write on a sticky note so you can refer back to them:

- You are not alone in your pain. God is right there with you. And his presence is better than out.
- I am created in the image of God. Regardless of how anyone has treated me, I am still his.
- Don't be overcome by evil, but overcome evil with good.

HAGAR
SESSION 7

On Your Own

Memory Verse

She gave this name to the Lord who spoke to her:
"You are the God who sees me."

(Genesis 16:13 NIV)

In Real Life:

DRAMA ACTIVITY: Out, Out, OUT

A businesswoman sits in her car and remembers a time twenty years ago when her son was small and God spoke to her through a situation in a car.

1 Have you ever just wanted out of a situation? If so, what was it about that situation that made *out* seem like the only viable solution?

2 Why didn't the woman in the drama get her son out of the car? Do you think she should have, or not? Looking back at your own situation, were there factors that now make sense that explain why you couldn't just get out?

3 Maybe you were able to get out of your tough situation. If so, how were the results satisfying or not satisfying? If not, what were the results of staying in?

4 What if God said to you right now, "You're right where you're supposed to be. And you're not alone. I am right here with you. And that's better than out"? Does having God with you in your current situation feel like it is enough for you? Why or why not?

5 What do you think it means to have God "with you" in a situation? What does he do and not do? (If it's helpful, you can look at John 14:16–17, 26–27.)

There are things about modern Western culture that make it harder for us to be aware of God with us. In a world inundated with artificial connections and online relationships, it is easy to think of ourselves as separate, at a distance from everything we think of as outside ourselves. For example, we think of our minds as separate from our bodies. An illness can happen to the body and we say, "I'm not letting it get to me," as if "me" is separate from "my body." We also think of ourselves as separate from the people around us. What happens to them doesn't

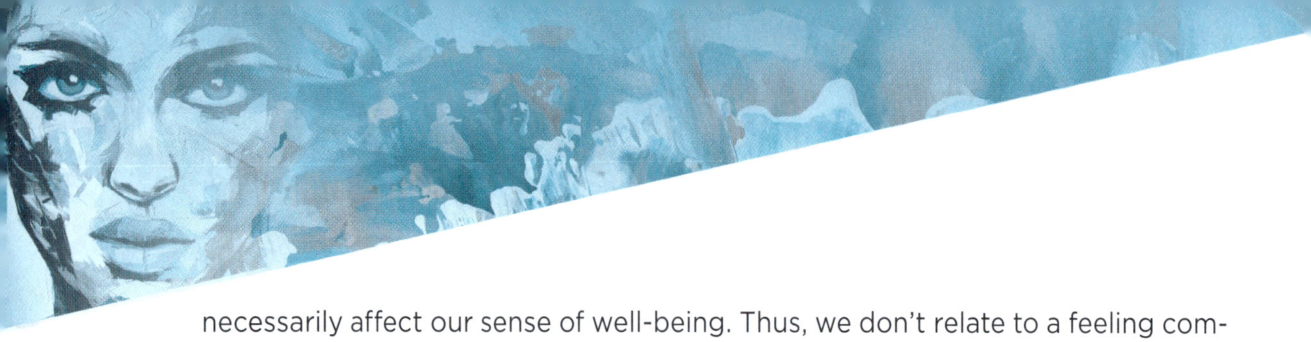

necessarily affect our sense of well-being. Thus, we don't relate to a feeling common in the ancient world and still common in Asian cultures today: the feeling of shame because someone in our family has brought shame on the family. In the West we think our family isn't "us." In the same way, we don't relate to the idea that we need to be part of a church family because God wants to relate to us as a community, not only as individuals. Many of us just want to experience God one-on-one. "Forget community, forget the body of Christ, just me and Jesus is all I need." But when we distance ourselves from our own bodies, from other people, from "the world" and the church, we inevitably hold God at a distance too. We think he's the one being distant, when in fact, it's us.

6 Do you hold other people at a distance? How does that play out in your daily life? How does it play out in the way you relate to a church community?

7 Do you think you hold God at a distance? What makes you think you do or you don't?

8 Spend some time praying through Psalm 46. Write down two to three things the psalm says to you about God's presence with you.

WHEN life does not **affirm** your *significance*, **God will.**

Authority Figures

CONNECTION ACTIVITY

Have you been hurt by someone in authority, in the church or elsewhere? If so, this exercise gives you a chance to process that experience and move into healing. Think about the person or people who hurt you. Write about the following:

What place of authority or position did they hold in your life? ______________

____

What did they do to hurt you or betray your trust? ______________________

____

Was there anyone else who was involved or aware of what was going on? If so, who? ____

____

How has this affected your life: your growth; your hurt; your isolation; your feelings of anxiety, fear, shame, anger, numbness; your understanding of yourself; your understanding of God? Have you grieved this hurt? Tell God how this made you feel. Ask God how it made him feel.

What is your part now? Where do you need to take ownership, make amends, reach out, forgive? Even if you feel that others were 99 percent to blame, is there 1 percent you can give toward reconciliation in heart? Reconciliation in person is ideal, but if that's not possible, can you do the work of forgiving with a friend or counselor, with the help of God's grace?

Do you resist doing your part now? If so, what is that voice of resistance inside you saying?

How can you use this part of your past to glorify God and do good to others in the future?

Hagar in the Bible

SCRIPTURE ACTIVITY

Look up Genesis 17:1-26 and read it.

Hagar was pregnant with Ishmael when she ran away. But after her encounter with the God who sees, she returned a different woman to Abraham and Sarah's household. When we next pick up the story, Hagar's son Ishmael is thirteen years old (Genesis 17:25). Many years have passed in the household of Abraham, Sarah, Hagar, and Ishmael. We're not told how the four of them got along.

1 The Bible doesn't tell us about those formative years for Hagar and Ishmael. What do you imagine life was like for Hagar as a slave in Sarah's household and as the mother of Abraham's son for those fourteen years? What might have been the hard parts? Any good parts?

2 What kind of father might Abraham have been to Ishmael? How might that have affected his relationship with Sarah?

3 Read Genesis 17:15–21 again. What does God promise for Sarah here? How will her life change when this happens?

4 How will this affect the now-teenage Ishmael?

5 How will Hagar's life be affected when Sarah gets pregnant?

6 Sarah chose to use Hagar as a surrogate mother and Abraham agreed. Neither this plan nor the consequences involved God's promise. Now, years later, God is fulfilling his promise to Abraham and giving him a son through Sarah. He doesn't choose Ishmael to inherit the promise; he chooses Isaac. What does this situation tell us about God? About human nature?

7 If you were Hagar, what would you say to God when you get the news that Sarah is pregnant? How would God's promise in verse 20 affect, or not affect, what you say?

Forgiveness

REFLECTION ACTIVITY

Merriam-Webster's top definition of forgiveness is "to stop feeling anger toward (someone who has done something wrong)." But this is not what the Bible means by forgiveness. In the Bible, forgiveness is a choice, and you can't choose to stop feeling a feeling. Rather, your feelings will change (perhaps over time) in response to the choices you make.

There are other misunderstandings of forgiveness that we should clear out of the way. First, forgiveness does not require you to forget the offense. You can't choose to forget. But unless you forgive, the memory stays intact and can be triggered years later at the same intensity. Time is not a healer; God is. He wants us to remember his faithfulness to us time and again until we know he is enough.

Second, forgiveness does not require you to deny that what happened was wrong or that you were deeply hurt. To the contrary, to begin the process of forgiveness one must give words to the offense, be shocked and angry at evil, and not rationalize it away. Third, you don't have to accept excuses for the other person's behavior.

Also, forgiveness doesn't ask you to trust the other person again. If the person has a pattern of wrong behavior, you should put boundaries around your relationship with her. If the other person establishes a new pattern of behavior, you can then choose to rebuild trust over time.

So if forgiveness doesn't ask all that of you, what does it ask? First of all, it asks you to let go of the demand that the other person pay for what she did. You renounce the desire for equal harm to come to the other person. You even renounce the demand for fairness. You accept that you have borne the high price for the wrongdoing by others, and you're not going to demand compensation. (If the person did something illegal, that's a separate issue. We're talking about interpersonal relationships.)

Second, forgiveness asks you to treat the other person with love. You may not have warm feelings toward her right away, but love means you *actively seek her good*. You look for opportunities to treat her with kindness and respect. You ask God to show you what will build her up, and you act on that insight. Feelings of compassion may follow your choice to act. If you're no longer in a relationship with the person, you can actively seek her good by praying for her and never speaking of her in a negative way.

The real fruit of forgiveness is that it allows us to approach new relationships with openness and love. When one person betrays our trust, it is easy to decide to stop trusting altogether. But forgiveness frees us from that stance. It moves us toward trustworthy people and gives them a chance to be part of our healing.

Forgiveness is good for us. When we hold onto resentment, it harms us much more than it harms the other person. We are the ones who stay stuck, when we could be living in freedom and love instead.

Forgiveness is often a process more than a one-time event. The questions in this section may only begin that process. They are intended to help you identify where you are getting stuck in forgiving.

The process of forgiveness often begins as you express your anger and hurt to God, perhaps in writing, and perhaps to another person as well. For example, what is the experience that you are struggling to forgive? What happened? What are you feeling? You may want to use the questions listed on pages 162–163 under "Authority Figures" (p. 162) to process the events and how they have affected you. If you are ready to go to the next step, then the questions in this exercise may be helpful to you.

1 What is holding you back from forgiving someone? Write down all your questions and reservations.

2 Do you resent God for allowing this person to hurt you? Describe your feelings toward God.

3 Read Matthew 18:21–35. A talent (verse 24) is a unit of money worth about twenty years' wages for a laborer. A denarius (verse 28) is worth one day's wage. What reason does this story give for why we should keep forgiving our brothers and sisters over and over?

4 Deep down, do you buy the claim that you owe God ten thousand talents' worth of debt? Take some time to write about how you have or haven't wronged God. Think about the fact that he created the universe, and everything in it belongs to him. Think about the fact that he made you, and he consistently gives you food and water and shelter no matter what your behavior is. Have you had a consistent attitude of thankfulness and respect for him, or have you taken his generosity for

granted, like you might deserve it? Have you consistently acknowledged his right to be in charge of your life, or have you tried to take control? Do you seek to follow his agenda or your own? Do you treat his people as Jesus treated them? (Do questions like these make you feel attacked or humbled?)

5 After reflecting on what you owe God, are you persuaded that he has forgiven you for more than what this other person owes you? Why or why not?

6 What will it cost you if you forgive the person who hurt you?

7 What will it cost you if you choose not to forgive?

Listening

PRAYER ACTIVITY

Write a letter to God about a hurt you have suffered because of someone else. Pour out your heart to him. He really wants to hear what's on your heart. If it's helpful, read Psalm 55. Use your private journal if you prefer.

Now write God's response. If you'd like, check out Psalm 34:18 and Luke 6:27–36.

HAGAR
SESSION 8

Transformed and Seen

Memory Verse

She gave this name to the Lord who spoke to her:
"You are the God who sees me."

(Genesis 16:13 NIV)

Select a volunteer
to read the following:

Have you ever felt invisible or insignificant in comparison with others? Perhaps you were the "good kid" in your family or classroom, where the troublemakers got all the attention. Maybe you've never fit in with the athletes, creatives, or intellectuals. Maybe your life feels less than Instagram-post worthy. Perhaps you've attended more weddings as a bridesmaid than years you've been alive and wonder when it will be your turn.

As a woman and a slave, Hagar was invisible in her culture. Yet when her life bottomed out, God spoke to her, and she realized God had seen her. That moment transformed her life. Being seen by God changed Hagar. Her circumstances were still far from ideal, yet she was able to handle them because she knew she was seen by a power greater than her circumstances. In this final study, we will explore what it means to be seen by God and how that affects the way we deal with an unknown future.

Check In

Before you dive into the video, take a few minutes to check in with each other. Let each person choose one of the following to respond to:

- What did you get out of the "On Your Own" activities you did for Session 7?
- If you could have God's full attention, what is one thing you would like to say to him?

Next, say your memory verse aloud together, along with its reference.

At a Glance: HAGAR

Age-old problem: Feeling insignificant

Age-old mistake: Overcompensating in word or deed to get attention

God's timeless wisdom: Rest, and respond in love, trusting that God sees you. Waiting and responding and trusting can be difficult. But God doesn't just see our external circumstances, he knows what is going on inside our hearts as well: *"O Lord, you have searched me and known me! You know when I sit down and when I rise up; you discern my thoughts from afar" (Psalm 139:1–2 ESV).*

Video Notes

Play the video segment for Session 8. It's about 28 minutes long. As you watch, use the following outline to record thoughts that stand out to you.

DRAMA: Nicole

I don't care what the owners think, I care what you think. I care what Katie thinks, and she's proud of me.

TEACHING: Kasey

God sees Hagar just because he wants to.

Hagar knows she is free, regardless of what does or does not change in her external circumstance.

Where are you hiding out? Where are you fearful? God sees you. Draw near.

TEACHING: *Jada*

Nothing you do, good or bad, surprises God or makes him love you less.

When you mess up, that's when you draw near to him.

The answer is him. It's his presence. That alone is enough.

Group Discussion

Leader, read each numbered prompt to the group.

1 In the drama, the diner manager says that ultimately she doesn't care what the diner owners think of her. She cares what God thinks and what her daughter thinks.

Whose opinion matters to you? Whose opinion actually affects what you do and how you feel about yourself? Is there a difference between the audience you're playing to and the audience you think you *should* be playing to?

2 What difference does it make to your life whether or not God sees you? Does it make any difference in what you do?

3 Kasey said the moment Hagar knew God saw her was the moment she was free inside, regardless of what did or didn't change about her external circumstance. Why do you think being seen has that effect?

4 God is right here, willing to grieve with us through the hard things of life. How do we take advantage of that offer?

5 Many people are unaware that God sees them. What do you think gets in the way of that awareness?

6 Jada said, "When you delight in the Lord, the Lord will deliver and rescue." What does it mean to delight in the Lord?

7 Take a minute on your own and write down your response to this question (you won't have to share your answer): On a scale of 0 to 5, how confident are you that you totally belong to God despite your popularity or platform in the world? Mark where you are on the continuum below.

0	1	2	3	4	5
Not at all confident					Very confident

Has anything changed for you since Session 5? If so, what?

8 Now share with the group: What are you grateful for that you've received from this study on Hagar? What will you take with you?

Select a volunteer
to read the following:

Hagar says to God, "You are the God who sees me." What does it mean to be seen by God? First, it means that the God who runs the universe notices us. He pays attention to us. We matter. Second, it means that he knows everything about us. We often don't see our past or our present as they really are, and we're completely blind to our future. God, on the other hand, sees the whole of our life through the lens of his sovereignty. He sees our strengths and weaknesses. He sees our virtues and faults. He sees the good and the bad, and he never turns away. He turns toward us in love. Third, it means he cares about our pain and our needs. He grieves with us when we feel scared or rejected. Fourth, it means he provides what we need (although not everything we want) to be at peace despite the painful circumstance or hurtful person. Finally, and most importantly, being seen by God means he gives us the opportunity to experience him and be satisfied by him, who is more beautiful and desirable than anything in our universe.

In preparation for the coming week, write one thing you want to gain from your study time:

(ex: hope for my future, a better understanding of who I am . . .)

Closing Prayer

Ask a volunteer to read this prayer aloud over the group:

Creator God, thank you that you see us. Thank you that we matter to you, that you grieve with us, that you provide for us. Thank you that you know us completely and still accept us. We want to take you up on your offer to know you as much as an infinite and infinitely desirable God can be known. We entrust our circumstances into your hands, and we ask you to care for our needs as you see best. And most of all, we ask for the awareness that your Presence goes with us, because you are our hearts' desire. In Jesus' name, amen.

Keep This Close

As you go on your way this week and end this study, here are some thoughts that you may want to save in your phone or write on a sticky note so you can refer back to them and remember them.

- God sees me in my pain and grieves with me.
- I never have to hide from God.
- When I delight in the Lord, he will deliver and rescue.

HAGAR
SESSION 8

On Your Own

Memory Verse

She gave this name to the LORD who spoke to her:
"You are the God who sees me."

(GENESIS 16:13 NIV)

In Real Life:

DRAMA ACTIVITY: Enough, Part 2

The diner manager returns with a new perspective because she has learned that her daughter is proud of her. She says she cares about what her daughter thinks of her and what God thinks.

1 Think to yourself about what the following say about the audiences you are performing for and how much you care about what they think:

- The way you present yourself and treat people when you are at work (Take a few minutes to cast your mind back to the last time you were at work and how you acted throughout the workday. If your work takes place at home, you can either answer accordingly or skip this item.)
- The way you present yourself and treat people when you are with family (Again, take a few minutes to picture some scenes with your family.)
- The way you present yourself and treat people when you are at church
- The way you behave, treat people, treat responsibilities when no one can see you except God

2 Who do you think God sees when he looks at you?

3 Read Psalm 139. Then focus on verses 1–6. Do you like being seen by God in this way?

What are the pluses?

What are the minuses?

4 Consider what the psalmist says about hiding in verses 7–12. Are you glad that God is there, whether you go to exalted places or dark places? Or does that give you some discomfort? Why?

5 How does knowing God sees you affect the importance you attach to whether others see you? How does it affect your concern for what they think of you? What would it look like to live for an audience of One?

Hagar in the Bible

SCRIPTURE ACTIVITY

Look up Genesis 21 and read it.

Ishmael was thirteen years old when God promised that Sarah would have a son the following year. So he was fourteen when Isaac was born, as Genesis 21:1–7 recounts. Then the story skips ahead to when Isaac was weaned (verse 8) at about age three. So that makes Ishmael about seventeen. He was not a tiny child and knew full well what was going on. And Hagar was no longer a young woman.

1 Abraham doesn't want to do what Sarah asks in verse 10, but God tells him to do it (verses 11–13). How might this be better for Hagar and Ishmael in the long run?

2 In the short run, though, it is very hard on Hagar and Ishmael. They go out into the semi-desert and run out of water. Ishmael gets faint from dehydration, and Hagar has to half-carry, half-drag him into the shade of a bush (verse 15). Then she goes far enough away that she doesn't have to watch him die, and she starts to weep loudly.

3 Have you ever been in a situation where you felt like that? If so, when? What did you do?

4 The name "Ishmael" means "God heard." The name appears nowhere in this chapter, but verse 17 begins with the same syllables: "God heard." This highlights the importance of the words. Why does it matter that God heard?

GOD is saying, "I see you, I know, and I'm with you. I am El Roi. Nothing catches me by *surprise*."

5 Consider what God does when he hears (verses 17–21). Do you believe God hears you like that? What helps you believe that? Or what gets in the way?

6 Ishmael wasn't the chosen son, the son of the promise. He was the son who was sent away, the son of a slave. And yet, verse 20 insists, "God was with the boy." Do you think that makes up for the rejection? Why or why not?

7 How do you respond to the way Hagar's story is left at the end? What are your thoughts and feelings?

8 What will you take away from the story of Hagar? What has it told you about God? About yourself? About life?

Journal Time

Choose *one* of the following topics to journal about:

- Jada said, "When you mess up, that's when you draw near to God. That's when you go to church, that's when you call for prayer. That's when you let your friends know what's going on. God never wants us to hide from him." Do you do these things when you mess up, or do you hide? What motivates you to do what you do? How helpful is what you do? If you face obstacles in doing what Jada recommends, how might you address those obstacles?
- Jada said, "Very often, we think that when God seeks us out, he's going to give us the answer we've been waiting for. But the truth is, the answer is him. It's his presence. That alone is enough." Is God's presence enough for you? Why or why not? How do you think we know when God's presence is with us? Is his presence with you? How important is intimacy with God to you, compared with the other things you want?
- What do you think it means to delight in God? What sorts of attitudes and behaviors do you think it involves? Do you delight in God? Why do you or don't you? How does delighting in God (or not delighting in him) affect your life?
- In Session 2 you thought about whether you believe God accepts you completely or whether you believe there are things you have to do to earn love. Where are you now with that? How has your study of Hagar helped you, or not helped you, with that?

Whichever topic you choose, finish up by writing about this question:

- What do I want to do differently in my day-to-day life as a result of this reflection?

Dialoguing with God

PRAYER ACTIVITY

Take some time to talk with God about delighting in him. What are some reasons you have for delighting in him? Tell him those. Then tell him about the things in your life that have been barriers to delight. You might talk with him about things you reflected on earlier in this study, such as ways people have hurt you, times you've felt rejected, shame and hiding, or feeling that you need to earn love. Tell him how much you need him to heal you in the place of your hurts and put you on a fresh path. Ask him to help you know that he fully accepts you as you are. Ask him to help you delight in him in the midst of whatever has happened to you in the past and whatever is going on in your life now. If it's helpful, write your prayer here.

Now, what do you think God might want to say in response? See, for example, Romans 9:25–26; Ephesians 5:1–2; Song of Solomon 2:8–15.

Welcome to Week 9

NAOMI

When I Feel Worthless, God Says I'm *Enough*

In chaos, GOD is our *constant*.

NAOMI
SESSION 9

When Hard Times Hit

Memory Verse

"I am the Lord your God,
who brought you up out of Egypt.
Open wide your mouth and I will fill it."

(Psalm 81:10 NIV)

Select a volunteer
to read the following:

Times of misery are inevitable in this life. Even in our society, with its advanced medical science, people still suffer and die. Sometimes death hits unexpectedly. Sometimes an illness persists for years with surgeries, treatments, symptoms, and perhaps the worst: uncertainty.

Other losses can be just as devastating: unemployment, divorce, rebelling children, unexpected expenses, substance abuse, disability, incarceration—the possibilities are endless. Such losses make us feel like we're wading through mud in an unknown territory and can't get our bearings. If you haven't yet experienced something that feels like a huge loss, you're probably familiar with smaller ones that can sting just as badly in the moment.

Have you felt like God is silent in these times? We wonder how he could allow such disasters. If God is so powerful and so good, why doesn't he change our circumstances or find a way to end our suffering? It's the age-old question, "Why does a good God allow bad things to happen?" But the truth is that in this broken world, in his sovereignty and grace, he allows suffering to afflict lots of people every day because he knows the end of the story—the good and perfect and whole end.

In this study we're going to be introduced to a woman named Naomi who lost her husband and both of her sons to death. She was so distraught she tried to change her name to "Bitter." But through a strange, yet sovereign, turn of events, Naomi found a way of dealing with her suffering without giving up her commitment to a God who was real and good. It took time. Things didn't get better overnight. But she found a way forward and went for it. She didn't stay stuck.

Check In

Welcome to the first session of Naomi: When I Feel Worthless, God Says I'm Enough. To get started, give everyone a chance to do the following:

- Share just three or four sentences about something or someone you've lost or some experience that has left you feeling worthless.

Take a minute on your own and write down your response to these questions (you won't have to share your answers):

→ Think of your emotional and spiritual life like your gas tank. On a scale of 0 to 5, with 0 being empty and 5 being full, how full is your tank today? Mark where you are on the continuum below.

0	1	2	3	4	5
empty					full

→ If your tank is not very full, how much *hope* do you have of its being full one day in the future? Can you look forward to a day when things will be a lot better than they are now, or do you see emptiness as far as the horizon? Mark your level of hope on the continuum below.

0	1	2	3	4	5
no hope					lots of hope

At a Glance: NAOMI

Where in Scripture: Ruth 1-4

Age-old problem: Loss and grief

Age-old mistake: Blaming God

God's timeless wisdom: Give voice to the depth of your pain, and keep trusting God at the same time. Consider how the psalmist claims his pain and struggle. He is honest about his frustration with God's lack of response—or so he thinks. He is basically calling God to the carpet, but then it's as if he remembers or recalls just who it is he is calling out to—God. Just a momentary lapse of reverence for who God is keeps us from trusting what he is capable of: *"O my God, I cry by day, but you do not answer, and by night, but I find no rest. Yet you are holy, enthroned on the praises of Israel" (Psalm 22:2–3 ESV).*

Video Notes

Play the video segment for Session 9. It's about 26 minutes long. As you watch, use the following outline to record thoughts that stand out to you.

DRAMA: *Nicole*

An art teacher moved cross-country after a divorce, and when she opened the boxes, everything was broken. Was God punishing her for ending her marriage?

TEACHING: *Jada*

Sometimes God will allow pain in your life to push you out of a place you shouldn't have been in to begin with.

In her hardest time, Naomi is still representing God well.

Does your life, even when it doesn't feel great, still make someone else want to choose God?

TEACHING: *Kasey*

A trauma to your brain is any time the experience is greater than your reality.

Let yourself lament. To lament is just to say out loud what you feel.

Pain is God's way of preparing us for our purpose and revealing his promise.

GOD doesn't **buy** our affections with *blessings*.

Group Discussion

Leader, read each numbered prompt to the group.

1. What stood out to you most from the video?

2. Kasey talked about lament. When we lament, we put words to the deep, internal grief we feel over the loss of something significant. How hard is it for you to lament? Have you ever allowed yourself to speak or write about your deepest feelings of sadness, loss, loneliness, fear, etc.?

3. Have you received help from believing Christians in painful past seasons? What feeling triggers at the thought of trusting Christian people with your pain?

4. Jada said God sometimes uses pain to push us out of a place that isn't good for us. What are some examples of situations that God might want to push us out of? How might pain be the thing that gets us out of those situations?

5 Naomi modeled faith in God so well that her daughter-in-law Ruth decided to abandon her culture and go with Naomi to follow this God. Think of the people who have modeled faith in God to you. What have they said, done, and been that has made God attractive or compelling?

6 Why do you suppose people often distance themselves from God when life gets hard? What assumptions about God and suffering does this distancing reflect?

7 What reasons do we have for staying faithful to God even when life is really hard?

8 How do you respond to the idea that if you're going through a dark season, you need to go to your local church and surround yourself with people who know God? How helpful does that sound to you, and why?

Select a volunteer

to read the following:

Some people think God exists to make them happy. They commit to him with the expectation that he will bless their health, their loved ones, their job, and everything else in their world. Yet, when he allows something to go horribly wrong, they feel betrayed.

While it's true that God does involve himself in our lives and that he will empower us to make good choices, he isn't necessarily interested in making sure our lives go smoothly according to our standards. Like a loving parent, God is much more interested in helping us become strong in character, loving toward others, and trusting toward him. Because we live in a world riddled with sin, he often allows us to endure terrible losses without giving us reasons why. Suffering happens to other people; why not to us? God doesn't buy our affections with blessings. He wants us to love him for himself regardless of our losses. Jesus is God in the flesh, and he came to earth and suffered horribly, partly so that we would know that he knows exactly what it's like to be human in a broken world. He understands what we're going through, and he's right here with us.

In preparation for the coming week, write one thing you want to gain from your study time:

(ex.: hope for my future, a better understanding of who I am . . .)

Closing Prayer

Ask for a volunteer to read this prayer aloud over the group:

Jesus, you know all the intimate details of the losses each one of us has suffered. You have allowed us to suffer in many ways with many unanswered questions. And yet we know that you are good and you hold our good in your heart. We also know that you have been on earth where we are and endured worse suffering than we can imagine. You know what it's like to be betrayed. You know what it's like to lose loved ones to death. You know what terrible physical suffering is like. You willingly endured the burden of the sin of every person on earth and the feeling of your Father's absence that this involved. And you are with us now in the midst of what we're going through. Please strengthen us to hold onto our faith, and empower us to make good decisions. Help us to trust you, even when we can't see the future. Please go with us, and lead us to the other side of what we're going through. In your name we pray, amen.

Keep This Close

As you go on your way this week, here are some thoughts from the video that you may want to save in your phone or write on a sticky note so you can refer back to them:

- Does your life, even when it's not great, still make someone want to choose God?
- When life is chaotic, God is your center point.
- Let yourself lament with the people who know your real name.

NAOMI
SESSION 9

On Your Own

Memory Verse

"I am the LORD your God,
who brought you up out of Egypt.
Open wide your mouth and I will fill it."

(PSALM 81:10 NIV)

Do your best to review the previous two memory verses as well: Jeremiah 1:5 and Genesis 16:13.

The point of This Memory Verse is that Naomi starts the story empty (Ruth 1:21), but she will end it full. So will we.

The psalmist is reminding his listeners of the way God rescued and provided for their ancestors. When their ancestors were slaves in Egypt, God did miracles to free them and bring them into a land of their own. God wants to provide for us in the same way. All we need to do, he says in verse 9, is to keep from bowing down to other gods. There are so many other tempting gods we could worship, like comfort, or money, control, sex, relationships, drugs. But all of these, if we make gods of them, will let us down. God pleads with us to believe his promise that he will provide for us if we worship only him. You'll have a chance to discuss this promise further in Session 10.

In Real Life:

DRAMA ACTIVITY: Broken, Part 1

The drama was about an art teacher who moved across the country after a divorce. When she opened the moving boxes, everything was broken. She wondered: Was God punishing her for ending her marriage? But then she remembered that God knew how hard she had tried to save her marriage. Still, though, when she looked at all the broken pieces of her life, she couldn't help thinking, *I wish I could fit in one of those boxes and just get thrown away.*

1 Have you ever wondered if God was punishing you? If so, what led you to wonder that?

Jesus took on himself the punishment we deserve (Romans 5:6–11). God doesn't send suffering on us to punish us; he allows it to remind us of who we really are. Jesus is in the fire with us—experiencing the flames with us. He mourns with us, hurts over our sufferings with us, and celebrates our victories with us. The hotter the flames burn, the closer he gets (Isaiah 43:2). Suffering shows our faith is genuine. It is being tested as fire tests and purifies gold: *"so that the tested genuineness of your faith . . . may be found to result in praise and glory and honor at the revelation of Jesus Christ" (1 Peter 1:7 ESV).*

2 Have you ever felt something like, "I wish I could fit in one of those boxes and just get thrown away"? Who is God to you when you are feeling like that? Is God someone you move toward or away from in a situation like that? Why?

3 Read Psalm 88. This is a psalm of lament. There are lots of psalms of lament in the book of Psalms, because the Jews thought that lament was important for individuals and for the gathered community of God's people. Which statements of lament in this psalm are especially meaningful for you?

4 How would you describe this psalmist's attitude toward God? What does he say *to* God and *about* God? Does he move toward or away from God?

5 Does the psalmist feel better by the end of the psalm? What does this say to you about the process of lament? About God's view of people who are lamenting?

6 Many psalms of lament contain expressions of trust in God and/or shouts of praise to God that he will deliver us. But this one doesn't. Why do you suppose 100 percent lament is included in the Bible?

Coping with Loss

CONNECTION ACTIVITY

In the video, Kasey named two effective ways to deal with loss and suffering: lament (on your own and with others) and spending time with God's people, who will help you stay pointed toward God. There are lots of other ways people try to deal with loss—some of them are constructive, and some are destructive. In this exercise, you'll have a chance to reflect on how you currently handle loss and what you want to do in the future.

1 First, describe the *feelings* and *thoughts* you are having in a season of loss or suffering. Feelings are things like anger, sadness, fear, joy, confusion, and numbness. If you're not sure what you feel, try probing around and putting words to it. You may be feeling several things. You may be feeling numb because your coping strategies are designed to tamp down unpleasant feelings. Complete these sentence starters and use the additional space if necessary.

I feel ____________________________________.

I feel like ________________________________.

I want to ________________________________.

I wish ____________________________________.

I'm hungry for ____________________________.

I think ___________________________________.

God seems like ___________________________.

2 What are some of the things you have done to try to cope with loss or suffering? List as many as you can think of. For example, maybe you eat, post or scroll on social media, get together with a friend, crawl into a cave, and so on.

3 Which of these coping strategies have been truly helpful?

4 Looking back, which strategies have been less than helpful, or downright harmful?

5 Do you seek numbness, an absence of negative feelings? If so, do you believe it's moving you forward? Explain.

Make an appointment with a friend to share your lament with her. Ask her if it's okay if you just pour out your heart uncensored about what you're going through. Don't have a friend you can talk to like that? Ask God to reveal her to you, because he promises she is there. Until then, consider talking with a professional counselor. Your group leader may be able to help you connect with one.

Naomi in the Bible

SCRIPTURE ACTIVITY

Look up Ruth 1 and read it.

This story takes place many centuries before the time of Jesus, when the nation of Israel was just getting started. Israel had not yet had a king. Instead, various parts of the country were ruled by people called judges (verse 1).

1 In both Moab and Israel at that time, there were few opportunities for women to work outside the home. Most women were supported by their male relatives. A widow without sons was looking at poverty. How do you think this fact influences what Naomi says and does in this chapter?

2 We aren't told why Ruth doesn't go home to her family and live with them until she can find another husband. What possible reasons can you think of?

3 What do you learn about Ruth's relationship with Naomi from what Ruth says in verses 16-17? What do her words suggest about each woman?

4 Have you ever been committed to someone like that? Have you ever had someone commit to you like that? If so, how has that commitment affected your life? What thoughts and feelings go through your mind when you think about Ruth's commitment?

5 In verse 20 (NIV) Naomi says, *"Don't call me Naomi,"* which means *pleasant*. Instead, she says, *"Call me Mara, which means bitter, because the Almighty has made my life very bitter."* To what extent do you think God is responsible for the bitterness of her life? Why?

6 What is your personal takeaway from this chapter of Ruth?

Journal Time

If you are going through something painful or are trying to come to terms with past suffering, it can be enormously helpful to pour out your thoughts and feelings on paper. You don't have to write it so that somebody else understands it; you just put down what's in you, however it comes out. You don't have to share any of it if you don't want to.

Choose *one* of the following topics to journal about:

- Have you ever felt like God has turned against you? Do you feel like that now? If so, describe the situation that is making you feel that way, and describe what you are feeling toward God. It's okay to say exactly what you feel, even if you're angry at God.
- Has God ever used pain to push you out of a place where you didn't need to be? If so, describe the place you were in and how God worked in your life to move you to a better place. Focus on how he used pain to motivate you. If you're in the situation right now, and you feel like God is trying to use pain to push you out of it, describe where you are and what better place you might go to.
- What is the loss or hardship you are currently struggling with? Describe what you're going through and the feelings you're having. If there's a history to it and it will help you to lay out the history, include that. If you have questions about what you should do, write those down.

Whichever topic you choose, finish up by writing about this question:

- What will you do differently in your day-to-day life as a result of this reflection? Use extra paper if necessary.

Listening

PRAYER ACTIVITY

For many of us, thoughts buzz around in our heads like flies, hard to capture and harder to quiet. For others, we have no idea what the thoughts in our heads do, because we're distracted all day long with people, tasks, entertainment, phone notifications, and social media. Our attention span is shorter than our pinky nail, and we feel comfortable only when something is occupying our attention.

God, however, seems to speak in the quiet. His voice is soft and low, so we don't hear him unless we're paying our full attention for a period of time. Giving our full attention is a skill that takes practice. We have to choose to slow down and endure the silence. At first, the silence can be uncomfortable. Thoughts and feelings arise that we might not want to deal with. Our minds run off on rabbit trails. We itch to grab our phones. However, if we persist in offering our stray thoughts to him, and settle back to listen, eventually we can learn to listen.

Take some time now to allow God the opportunity to speak to you. Find a quiet place where you can be alone. Turn off your phone—or better still, leave it somewhere else so it doesn't draw your eye and your thoughts. Lay before him your thoughts and feelings about your losses. Then let the busyness of your thoughts go.

If you find your mind drifting, easily distracted, or you're struggling to find downtime in your life, try reading Psalm 31, and listen to what God is saying to you there. God speaks to us in his Spirit. The Spirit is activated through the stimulus of truth. Don't be discouraged if you don't hear an audible message from God. He is always speaking to you through his Holy Word.

Sometimes it helps to read aloud or change up your surroundings. Take a walk, sit on the porch, head to the nearest park bench, or simply sit in your car alone for a few minutes if necessary.

NAOMI
SESSION 10

Behind the scenes

Memory Verse

"I am the Lord *your God,*
who brought you up out of Egypt.
Open wide your mouth and I will fill it."

(Psalm 81:10 NIV)

Select a volunteer

to read the following:

Loss can make you feel hopeless and worthless. Naomi's culture told her that her worth was tied to being a wife and mother of sons, and now she was neither. She had no status in the community and no means of earning a living. She felt hopeless and powerless in her circumstances, and when she decided to return home it was with an attitude to protect and defend herself. Yet she didn't know that the God of hope was already at work.

Hope is wanting something you don't have or wanting something to happen that hasn't happened. Biblical hope is wanting something you can't yet see but can be confident it will come in the future. The Bible spells out the glory we can hope for beyond this life, and that hope is an anchor when life sets our boats adrift. But what can you confidently hope for in this life? Is God at work in your here and now? How?

In this study you will see that God was already working behind the scenes of Naomi's life, long before she saw the fulfillment of things she couldn't bring herself to even hope for. He is working behind the scenes in your life too. By choosing not to define yourself by your current life circumstances, you can get in on something amazing.

Check In

Before you dive into the video, take a few minutes to check in with each other. Let each person choose one of the following to respond to:

- What did you get out of the "On Your Own" activities you did for Session 9?
- Where did you live before the place where you live now? How was it different from where you live now? How were you different, or not different?

Next, say your memory verse aloud together. Be sure to say the verse reference after it. If you don't know the verse from memory yet, read it with the group from page 217.

Practice reciting your previous two memory verses before moving on (hint: Jeremiah 1:5 and Genesis 16:13).

At a Glance: NAOMI

Age-old problem: Feeling of emptiness

Age-old mistake: Losing hope that things can change

God's timeless wisdom: Take action on the things you have the power to influence, and pin your hope on God's never-failing love for the rest: *"But the eyes of the LORD are on those who fear him, on those whose hope is in his unfailing love" (Psalm 33:18 NIV).*

Video Notes

Play the video segment for Session 10. It's about 17 minutes long. As you watch, use the following outline to record thoughts that stand out to you.

DRAMA: Nicole

Losing the thing you love more than life itself often reveals your deepest struggle.

TEACHING: Jada

Providence: "A timely preparation for future eventualities"

Many times we see God's providence before his provision.

Harvest is not just about the availability of food; it's about the abundance of food.

When you choose to define yourself by your life circumstances, you can miss out on the calling God has for you.

Where am I on this spectrum from pleasant to bitter?

How many divine moments have we missed because we have chosen to define ourselves by our life circumstances?

GOD is **working** behind the *scenes* in your life, **too.**

Group Discussion

Leader, read each numbered prompt to the group.

1 What stood out to you most from the video?

2 In the drama, the mother whose daughter ran away said, "Losing the thing you love more than life itself often reveals your deepest struggle. Mine was with God. Would I trust God if I couldn't control the outcome?" How do you typically deal with important situations when you can't control the outcome?

3 Naomi looked at her circumstances and wanted to rename herself "Bitter." She was defining herself by her circumstances. What's wrong with doing that?

4 Naomi thought God was against her, but he was working in her life in ways she didn't expect and couldn't imagine. How does God work in our lives in ways we don't expect? Give an example.

5 How easy is it for you to believe that God is at work behind the scenes in your life now? What helps you believe that? What gets in the way?

6 When Naomi decided to go home to the land where God was, God led Naomi to a place of harvest, of abundance. What would it mean for you to "go home to the land where God is"? (It may or may not be a physical place.)

7 Complete this sentence with something that you know God has done for you in the past:
I am the Lord your God who __________________________________.

8 To "open wide your mouth" means to ask God. Can you believe that if you ask, God will fill your mouth? If not, what is keeping you from believing it? If you do believe it, what will listening to him and following his ways look like in your case?

Select a volunteer

to read the following:

Jada quoted your memory verse:

"I am the LORD your God,
who brought you up out of Egypt.
Open wide your mouth, and I will fill it."
(Psalm 81:10 NIV)

Here the psalmist says that just as God freed the Israelites from slavery in Egypt generations ago, so also he can and will satisfy the needs of their descendants in the present day. All we need to do, as he says in the rest of the psalm, is to listen to him and follow his ways. She also quoted the following verse:

May the God of hope fill you with all joy and peace
in believing, so that by the power of the Holy Spirit
you may abound in hope. (Romans 15:13 ESV)

This passage says God wants to fill us with joy and peace and make us abound in hope. All we need to do is believe him.

In preparation for the coming week, write one thing you want to gain from your study time:

(ex.: hope for my future, a better understanding of who I am . . .)

Closing Prayer

Ask for a volunteer to read this prayer aloud over the group:

God of heaven and earth, you are the God of the harvest. You are the one who provides for us not just a little but abundantly. Sometimes that's hard for us to believe when we're living through a period of famine, when we feel empty and have no idea where what we need is going to come from. But you are the God who works behind the scenes to bring events together that we can't foresee. Please help us to listen to you, trust you, and follow your ways, and give us the courage to open wide our mouths so that you will fill them. We need your joy, your peace, your hope. We need some very concrete things. Please provide for each one of us. In Jesus' name, amen.

Keep This Close

As you go on your way this week, here are some thoughts from the video that you may want to save in your phone or write on a sticky note so you can refer back to them:

- "Courage is fear that has said its prayers."—C. S. Lewis
- When you choose to define yourself by your life circumstances, you can miss out on the calling God has for you.
- Even before you see things work themselves out, God is working behind the scenes.

NAOMI
SESSION 10

On Your Own

Memory Verse

"I am the Lord your God,
who brought you up out of Egypt.
Open wide your mouth and I will fill it."

(Psalm 81:10 NIV)

Do your best to review the previous two memory verses as well: Jeremiah 1:5 and Genesis 16:13.

In Real Life:

DRAMA: Letting Go

This session's drama is about a mother who found pills in her teenage daughter's backpack. She was overcome by fear and went wild trying to find out whether her daughter was using drugs. She tried to control things about her daughter's life to the point where her daughter eventually ran away. Then the mother learned some crucial things about herself and where to go from there.

1 What, for you, is the equivalent of finding pills in your daughter's backpack? What has upended your world?

2 How are you trying to deal with this? What specific things have you done?

3 When you look at the specifics of what you've done, do you find yourself, like the mom in the drama, trying to control the outcome? Has fear made you do anything? If so, what have been the results so far? Think about the effects on you, on the situation, and on others.

4 When you think about trusting God with this situation, what goes through your mind?

5 Read Psalm 130. This is another psalm of lament. But in this case, lament doesn't take up the whole poem. Instead, the poet spends some time taking his eyes off his circumstances and putting them on God. What does he say that is definitely lament?

6 What does he tell himself about God?

In verses 5–6, he says what he has decided to do. A little background may help. Watchmen stood on the walls of a city at night, looking out into the wild lands beyond and watching for the stealthy approach of enemies. Because they're up for hours at night and on their feet, with danger constantly on their minds, they passionately wait for morning, when they can get something to eat and go to bed.

7 Why do you suppose waiting for God like this (verses 5–6) is such an important part of a smart response to situations that turn our worlds upside down? How could waiting be so important? What happens when we wait for God? How does waiting affect us?

8 What would waiting for God look like in your current situation? What would you stop doing? What would you keep doing?

SCRIPTURE ACTIVITY

Look up Ruth 2 and read it.

A little background will help you understand what's going on in this chapter. First, remember from the end of Ruth chapter 1 that it is the beginning of the barley harvest. All of the field workers around Bethlehem will go to their bosses' fields and begin harvesting barley. They will cut down the tall stalks of barley and gather them into bundles for transport. They will work as quickly and efficiently as possible, but inevitably in their haste they will leave behind a few stalks, especially at the edges of the fields. A landowner who is most concerned about his profit will then send a worker or two into his field to *glean* it—that is, to carefully cut and gather all of the remaining stalks so that nothing is wasted. But God's law says that instead, landowners should allow the poor people in the neighborhood to glean their fields (Leviticus 23:22). Harvesting barley is hard, backbreaking work, and this law allows the poor who own no land and have no job to do real work and get enough to eat. It is God's law, but there are no police to enforce it, so it depends on social custom and the conscience of the individual landowner.

Naomi and Ruth are poor. As women, they have almost no opportunity to get work. In Ruth 2:2, Ruth offers to go to a field and glean it so they will have barley to eat.

Next, it's helpful to understand why in Ruth 2:8–9 Boaz tells Ruth to keep working in his field and to stay close to his female workers. In that culture, women without men to protect them are extremely vulnerable to sexual assault.

Boaz imagines what might happen to Ruth in someone else's field, and he takes steps to protect her.

Finally, in verse 20 Naomi tells Ruth that Boaz *"is a close relative of ours, one of our redeemers" (ESV).* A redeemer in Naomi's culture is a male relative who is expected to take action for a relative in need of justice or help. A redeemer is responsible for avenging a relative's murder, buying his property so that it won't be sold outside the family, and so on.

1 What does God's law about gleaning tell you about God? What is your opinion about it?

2 We don't see much of Naomi in this chapter, but she gives guidance to Ruth in verse 20. What does she say and do? What does this say about her? Could this indicate a change in Naomi's attitude?

3 Jada spoke about providence in this session's video. Where do you see God's providence at work in Ruth chapter 2?

4 How is God already at work addressing Naomi's emptiness and bitterness?

5 Where do you expect the story to go from here?

6 When you think about your own situation, how does this part of Naomi's story affect you?

Journal Time

Choose *one* of the following topics to journal about:

- Have you been defining yourself by your circumstances? If so, what definition or identity have you been wearing? How has that affected your thoughts, feelings, and actions? How *would* you like to define yourself?
- Where might God be at work in your life right now behind the scenes? How might he be trying to lead you to a place of harvest? How can you best cooperate with him?
- Where are you right now on the spectrum from pleasant (5) to bitter (0)? Are you mad at God? Do you feel like he owes you, that he's left you empty? Journal your honest feelings. Then ask yourself how you're going to respond. Are you going to be defined by your current life situation and emotions? Or are you going to ask God if he has something greater in store? Do you believe that even in your hunger and hopeless feelings, the God of the harvest can create a hopeful situation?

Whichever topic you choose, finish up by writing about this question:

- What will you do differently in your day-to-day life as a result of this reflection? How will this change your conversations, your prayer life, what you say to your friends, how you deal with your problems?

Listening

PRAYER ACTIVITY

You understand that you shouldn't define yourself by your circumstances, so how should you define yourself? Your deepest identity is not in how well your life is going, how much money you have, what you do for a living, whether you have children, or what your gender or ethnicity is. Your deepest identity is being a child of God, a member of God's family. You are far from worthless; you are enough as you are because God has made you enough.

Spend some time praying over 1 John 3:1–2 below:

See what kind of love the Father has given to us, that we should be called children of God; and so we are. The reason why the world does not know us is that it did not know him. Beloved, we are God's children now, and what we will be has not yet appeared; but we know that when he appears we shall be like him, because we shall see him as he is. (ESV)

In a private journal, write out a prayer to God, asking him to show you what it looks like to define yourself as his child. What does a child of God desire? What is unimportant to a child of God? What does a child of God fear, and not fear? What makes a child of God feel valuable at the end of the day? How does a child of God deal with other people's expectations? How does a child of God think about circumstances that aren't going so well? Ask God to give you a vivid picture of what your life is about as his child. Ask him to show you how he wants you to deal with your circumstances. When you're ready, write down three things you are thankful for in all of this.

NAOMI
SESSION 11

Better Than Being Fixed

Memory Verse

"I am the L*ORD your God,*
who brought you up out of Egypt.
Open wide your mouth and I will fill it."

(Psalm 81:10 NIV)

Select a volunteer

to read the following:

There are lots of reasons why you may be reluctant to be honest with God and those close to you about your pain, fear, anger, and confusion. You may have been taught that God wants you to *"rejoice in the Lord always" (Philippians 4:4 NIV)*, and that sounds like "Lament to the Lord never." You may have been ridiculed or ignored as a child when you cried. Your pain may feel so huge that you can't imagine anyone being able to handle it and continue to respect you as an adult. You may be so angry at God that you don't want to get near him. You may fear that someone will respond to your honesty by trying to fix your emotions and your situation, instead of truly listening to you. All of these are understandable reasons for not being honest, and yet honesty is vital for a life with God.

God's perspective on Naomi's life was that he was providentially working behind the scenes of her life to bring her emptiness to fullness. He had heard her lament, and he was responding. Our human perspective often blinds us to his work and makes us doubt that our lament could make any difference. But as we will hear in this study, we need to know that we have a God we can cry out to even in our confusion, a God who accepts us and tells us the truth about who we really are.

Check In

Before you dive into the video, take a few minutes to check in with each other. Give everyone a chance to respond to the following:

- What did you get out of the "On Your Own" activities you did for Session 10?
- When you were a child, what were you taught to do when you were hurt? Or what did you learn to do without being directly taught?

Next, say your memory verse aloud together. Be sure to say the verse reference with it and don't forget to return to your first two memory verses!

At a Glance: NAOMI

Age-old problem: Loss and grief

Age-old mistake: Hide the pain from others and from God

God's timeless wisdom: Let others be drawn to you by the honesty with which you deal with loss in the presence of God: *"As for me, I am poor and needy, but the Lord takes thought for me. You are my help and my deliverer; do not delay, O my God!" (Psalm 40:17 ESV).*

Video Notes

Play the video segment for Session 11. It's about 17 minutes long. As you watch, use the following outline to record thoughts that stand out to you.

DRAMA: Nicole

A mom speaks about life after her son has graduated from high school.

I will turn my tassel too. I promise.

TEACHING: Kasey

Trusting God is not going to fix us. It's going to tell us the truth about who we are.

Naomi's God was not trying to fix her. He did not need anything from her.

We will never trust God standing outside the flames.

Are you attractive to other people? Do other people want to be around you because they connect to you, because you openly share your pain with them?

Ruth watched Naomi walk through the fire with a God that Naomi could cry out to, come to, be angry with, be confused by.

Group Discussion

Leader, read each numbered prompt to the group.

1. What stood out to you most from the video?

2. Kasey says trusting God is not going to fix us. It's going to tell us the truth about who we are: women accepted by God. What do you think is wrong with wanting God or someone else to fix us?

3. Do you know deeply that you are accepted by God? How does knowing it affect the way you feel about yourself and the way you interact with others? Or how does not knowing it affect how you feel and what you do?

4. How do you think a person gets to know that she is fully, completely accepted by God? Are there things she does or doesn't do? Are there things that happen to her? Are there things that other people do or don't do?

5 Kasey said Naomi had a God she could cry out to, come to, be angry with, be confused by. A God who wasn't trying to fix her. Do you have a God like that? Or do you see God differently? Describe how you see God.

6 Has suffering caused you to focus on yourself and shut others out? Or has it turned your heart to hear the needs in others' cries? Describe how it's done one or the other, or some of each, or something else.

7 What do you think makes the difference between someone getting isolated, bitter, or destructive because of suffering, or someone getting transformed and moved to reach outward to others because of suffering? Are there things other people can do that draw the person in one direction or the other? Are there choices the person makes? Is it something God needs to do that the person receives or doesn't receive?

The change in deeply ingrained **habit patterns** takes **TIME**.

Select a volunteer
to read the following:

Trusting God begins a process of transforming us to become like Jesus in our character (2 Corinthians 3:18). It increasingly improves our ability to treat other people well (Galatians 5:22–23). Also, if we have more trust, we may have less anxiety. And if we deeply believe God accepts us, we will probably feel less shame. But trusting God isn't a quick and automatic solution to unpleasant emotions and relationship difficulties. Nor does it necessarily resolve the problems in our circumstances. So it doesn't necessarily make us feel good. And the change in deeply ingrained habit patterns takes time. Some aspects of our personality may not change in this lifetime. This is what we mean when we say that trusting God doesn't "fix" us.

In preparation for the coming week, write one thing you want to gain from your study time:

(ex.: hope for my future, a better understanding of who I am . . .)

Closing Prayer

Ask for a volunteer to read this prayer aloud over the group:

Creator God, we are so grateful that you have created a place for us to honestly explore these hard questions. Thank you that you are a God we can cry out to, be angry with, and be confused by—and still you are our loving God. A God who totally accepts us the way we are now and isn't trying to fix us so that we "behave." Please be the bedrock Presence in our lives who holds and carries us through seasons of suffering. Please use that suffering to move us out of business as usual and into a life that is offered for the good of others. Please heal in us the harmful effects of past and present suffering that have hardened our hearts in big and small ways. Please give us the courage to move toward others honestly with freedom and joy. We pray this in Jesus' name, amen.

Keep This Close

As you go on your way this week, here are some thoughts from the video that you may want to save in your phone or write on a sticky note so you can refer back to them:

- Trusting God is going to tell us the truth about who we are.
- We need a God we can cry out to, come to, be angry with, be confused by. A God who isn't trying to fix us.

NAOMI
SESSION 11

On Your Own

Memory Verse

"I am the Lord your God,
who brought you up out of Egypt.
Open wide your mouth and I will fill it."

(Psalm 81:10 NIV)

Do your best to review the previous two memory verses as well: Jeremiah 1:5 and Genesis 16:13.

In Real Life:

DRAMA ACTIVITY: Turning the Tassel

In the drama, a mom speaks about her feelings after her son has graduated from hi school. She refers to the moment when he moved the tassel on his mortarboard fro one side to the other.

1 In what ways is the drama a modern-day lament?

2 The mom in the drama talked about "that deep, sinking feeling of being left." Have you ever felt that feeling? If so, what was that like for you?

3 How has that affected who you are today?

4 Read Psalm 22:1-11. This is another psalm of lament, though later it does get around to promising to praise God for deliverance (verses 25-31). But let's not move too quickly to the praise. In verses 1-11, what negative feelings and thoughts does the psalmist express honestly?

5 What does the psalmist remind himself about God (verses 3-5, 9-10)?

6 Does any of what he tells himself about God help you face your own current situation? If so, what?

7 How is this psalm like the way you talk to God? How is it different?

8 What do you want to say to God as a result of this reflection?

SCRIPTURE ACTIVITY

Look up Ruth 3 and read it.

Once again, a little knowledge of customs in Naomi's culture will help you follow the story. First, in Ruth 3:2 (NIV), Naomi says Boaz *"is winnowing barley tonight at the threshing floor."* Winnowing was a way of separating kernels of grain from dirt and from the papery chaff that encased them. The workers loosened the barley kernels from the straw stalks and spread the kernels on a wide flat area called a threshing floor. Then with winnowing fans they tossed the kernels into the air, and the wind blew away the lighter dirt and chaff. The heavy kernels fell to the ground. A threshing floor was always laid out in an open area where the maximum available wind was likely to blow.

Next, Ruth again calls Boaz a "redeemer" (3:9). One of the responsibilities of a dead man's near relative in this culture is to marry his widow and have a child to carry on his family line. Deuteronomy 25:5–10 says it is the responsibility of the late husband's brother, but Ruth's late husband has no living brother, and the book of Ruth suggests that another near relative has the option of doing the job. He isn't obliged to do it by law, but he can do it as an act of generosity toward his kin. That is what Naomi is hoping for when she sends Ruth to Boaz.

1 What do you think of Naomi's plan in Ruth 3:1–4? What do you think Ruth is risking by doing what Naomi says? Why does Naomi think the risk is worthwhile?

2 When Ruth identifies herself to Boaz in verse 9 and then asks him to act as a redeemer, he says, *"May you be blessed by the Lord, my daughter. You have made this last kindness greater than the first in that you have not gone after young men, whether poor or rich" (verse 10 ESV).* To whom do you think she is being kind by not going after young men? Why do you think that?

3 If you were to create Boaz's social media profile, what would you write?

4 Where do you see God at work behind the scenes in this episode of the story?

5 What can this episode teach us about the ways we cooperate with God in addressing the challenges in our lives?

6 What do you expect will happen in the final episode of this story? Why do you expect that?

Journal Time

Choose *one* of the following topics to journal about:

- Kasey said, "It is painful saying no to something we have grown to love." What is that thing or person that you have grown to love but that isn't consistent with your best self? What does it give you that motivates you to cling to it? How is it causing harm? What would saying no to it involve? What help do you need to do that?
- What is suffering doing to you? Who have you become because of this pain? What do you like about who you have become, and/or what don't you like? Who would you like to be? How would you like to affect others? What will it take for you to get there? What help will you need?
- Are you attractive to other people? Do other people want to be around you because they connect to you, because you openly share your pain and hardship with them? Why do you suppose that's the case? How does that manifest in your life? If you're not a person who other people connect with, what do you think it would take for you to get there?
- How real is it to you that God fully and totally accepts you? What helps you believe that? What gets in the way? How do you think God sees you? Where did you get that perception? What do you need from God that might help you believe that he fully accepts you?

Whichever topic you choose, finish up by writing about this question:

- What will you do differently in your day-to-day life as a result of this reflection? Again, use extra paper if necessary.

Listening

PRAYER ACTIVITY

Write God a letter expressing your uncensored feelings about him and your current situation. This can be completely from your human perspective without regard for what you think you should be feeling or thinking. If you're in a really positive place, that's great. If you're in a really negative place, remember that's not a problem for God.

Dear God,

Now write some things about God that you know are true, based on what you've read in the Bible or heard taught or experienced for yourself. Write things that are relevant to what you wrote above. If you can't think of anything, look at the way Psalm 22 alternates between a candid expression of the psalmist's feelings and situation on the one hand, and what he knows about God on the other.

God, I know it's true that you . . .

If you have time, write what you think God might want to say back to you. For ideas, see Hebrews 2:14–18; 4:15–16; 5:7–9; and Psalm 91.

Daughter,

Congratulations and Well Done!

As you enter this final week of study, may this final message from Naomi be a blessing and deep encouragement to you.

NAOMI
SESSION 12

From Bitter to Blessed

Memory Verse

"I am the L*ORD your God,*
who brought you up out of Egypt.
Open wide your mouth and I will fill it."

(Psalm 81:10 NIV)

Select a volunteer

to read the following:

We often have a very narrow perspective when we look at our lives. Our attention is consumed by what we feel at the moment and how hard circumstances are crowding in on us. We can't see options for action, or other people's needs, or what God might be doing behind the scenes. Our whole story is us and our pain. That was the case for Naomi at the beginning of the book of Ruth. But Naomi chose not to give up on God, and she chose to care about the needs of Ruth. Now in this final study we will see the harvest of her perseverance.

Like Naomi, we too are part of a much bigger story that God has been telling for millennia, a story about God creating the world, pronouncing it good, then getting involved as it began to go wrong and reaching out to set it right. We can't see the entire role God wants us to play in his big story, but we can choose to trust him day after day after day. And we can choose to involve ourselves in the needs of other people. As Naomi did this, she went from bitter to blessed, from loneliness to legacy. That beautiful transformation is available for us too.

Check In

Before you dive into the video, take a few minutes to check in with each other. Let each person choose one of the following to respond to:

- What did you get out of the "On Your Own" activities you did for Session 11?
- How has someone else been a blessing to you? It could be a recent incident or something that happened a long time ago. Try to limit the story to about one minute.

Next, say your memory verse aloud together, along with its reference.

At a Glance: NAOMI

Age-old problem: Unmet needs

Age-old mistake: Thinking only of yourself and how to get your needs met

God's timeless wisdom: Focus on helping others to get their needs met, and trust that God will meet your needs in the process: *"Give, and it will be given to you. A good measure, pressed down, shaken together and running over, will be poured into your lap. For with the measure you use, it will be measured to you" (Luke 6:38 NIV).*

Video Notes

Play the video segment for Session 12. It's about 19 minutes long. As you watch, use the following outline to record thoughts that stand out to you.

DRAMA: Nicole

The art teacher from Session 9 reflects back on what happened a few weeks after all of her belongings showed up broken in her new home.

TEACHING: Jada

Many times our blessing comes after we have facilitated the blessing of someone else.

God can give you legacy beyond what you expected because it's all about his glory.

You don't need to decide who you are. God decided who you were before you were born.

TEACHING: *Kasey*

God is going to give you an opportunity to serve in the midst of your pain because the surefire antidote to anxiety, isolation, and depression is to serve others.

Choose to trust God over and over and over again until you feel it.

YOU, too, can have the **great** *reversal.*

Group Discussion

Leader, read each numbered prompt to the group.

1. Is God gathering up the shards of your broken life and making something new? Share something new he has done.

2. Naomi's blessing came after she made an effort to see that Ruth was blessed. How can we facilitate the blessing of someone else? What opportunities do we have?

3. What obstacles do we face in making our lives about helping others?

4 Peter said God's divine power has granted to us all things that pertain to life and godliness (2 Peter 1:3). Yet Peter was then arrested and slowly and brutally executed. His need for physical well-being was taken away. So what did Peter mean when he said that God has granted us all things that pertain to life and godliness?

5 What is a step of abiding in Christ that you could take in your current situation?

6 Share with the group: What are you grateful for that you've received from this study on Naomi? What will you take with you?

Spend time with JESUS, drink him in. This is where real *satisfaction* comes from.

7 Take a minute on your own to write down your response to these questions (you won't have to share your answers):

Think of your emotional and spiritual life like your gas tank. On a scale of 0 to 5, with 0 being empty and 5 being full, how full is your tank today? Mark where you are on the continuum below.

0	1	2	3	4	5
empty					full

If your tank is not very full, how much *hope* do you have of its being full one day in the future? Can you look forward to a day when things will be a lot better than they are now, or do you see emptiness as far as the horizon? Mark your level of hope on the continuum below.

0	1	2	3	4	5
no hope					lots of hope

Select a volunteer to read the following:

Kasey said freedom is abiding in Christ. That's Christian language from the Bible, but what does it mean? First, to abide means to endure, to last a long time. It also means to dwell. Dwelling in connection to Christ is a way of life that we need to begin to practice so that over time it becomes a habit, day after day.

Second, Bible teacher Sinclair Ferguson says, "Abiding in Christ means allowing His Word to fill our minds, direct our wills, and transform our affections."[†] It means to bet our lives daily on Jesus' love for us that he displayed on the cross. It means to increasingly love others (with his help) because we love him. It means to trust him moment by moment, especially in hard times, letting the pain strip away everything false and reveal the persons we were meant to be. It means to spend time with Jesus, to drink him in. This is where real satisfaction comes from.

† Sinclair Ferguson, "What Does It Mean to Abide in Christ?" Ligonier Ministries, February 19, 2018, https://www.ligonier.org/blog/what-does-it-mean-abide-christ/.

In preparation for the coming week, write one thing you want to gain from your study time:

(ex.: hope for my future, a better understanding of who I am . . .)

Closing Prayer

Ask for a volunteer to read this prayer aloud over the group:

Loving God, thank you that you are transforming us from bitter to blessed. Thank you that we can trust you with our circumstances, because we know that when we are not in control—you are. You have already given us everything we need for life and intimacy with you, so help us abide in these things, as they are enough. Continue to tune our hearts to the cries of others so that we might contribute to their transformation and healing. Please keep us connected to you, drawing strength from you every day. Thank you for what you are doing in us, seen and unseen. All of these requests we bring to you in Jesus' name, amen.

Keep This Close

As you go on your way this week, here are some thoughts from the video that you may want to save in your phone or write on a sticky note so you can refer back to them:

- Many times our blessing comes after we have facilitated the blessing of someone else.
- In our suffering there is a choice. We can choose to trust God over and over and over again.

NAOMI
SESSION 12

On Your Own

Memory Verse

"I am the Lord your God,
who brought you up out of Egypt.
Open wide your mouth and I will fill it."

(Psalm 81:10 NIV)

As you end this study, take these three memory verses with you, letting them remind you always that you are known by God: Jeremiah 1:5, Genesis 16:13, Psalm 81:10.

In Real Life:

DRAMA ACTIVITY: Broken, Part 2

The art teacher from Session 1 reflects back on a work of art she received as a gift. It was made up of the broken shards of stained glass from her disastrous moving experience. A picture of God's redeeming love.

1. Think of the broken shards of your life that God is shaping into a new work of art. Have you begun to glimpse the new work that God is making? What can you see? What can't you see?

2. How tempted are you, like the art teacher, to throw away all the broken pieces of what has been shattered? What would you miss by doing that?

3 Psalm 40 is a psalm with a lot of celebration and yet still some lament. This poet is grateful for what God has done for him, but he still has real desperation that hasn't been tied up in a bow. In verses 1–3, what has God done for this poet?

4 Read verses 11–17. What is still going on in the poet's life?

5 All of that is still going on in his life, and yet the poet is able to celebrate God. What does this say about his view of his life and of God?

6 In these four sessions we have looked at four approaches to lament, from pure honesty about how bad things are to a mix of gratitude and outcry for help. In a messy and honest spiritual life, we can move back and forth among these. What is most helpful for you in your current state? Offer a prayer to God that expresses where you are right now.

Naomi in the Bible

SCRIPTURE ACTIVITY

Look up Ruth 4 and read it.

The first scene takes place at the town gate. This was the main entrance to the town, and it was where the elders spent their time and where legal matters were settled. It was a good location for public business because people heading out to their fields or home from their fields had to pass through the gate.

In verses 1–6, the other redeemer isn't named. Israelite tradition won't let him buy Elimelech's land unless he also takes Elimelech's widowed daughter-in-law, Ruth. But Israelite custom will reckon her firstborn son not as the legal son of her new husband but as the legal son of her late husband. The new husband will pay all the expense of buying the land, feeding Ruth and Naomi, and raising the son, but as soon as the son is an adult, he will inherit Elimelech's land. And if Ruth has more children, the new husband will have to include them as his heirs along with the children he already has. He probably already has a wife and children, and so doesn't want to dilute his estate in this way.

Boaz may have more money than his kinsman, so he can afford to support Ruth, Naomi, and whatever children Ruth may have.

1 How do the events of chapter 4 affect Naomi?

2 In chapter 1, Naomi asked the women of her Bethlehem community to call her "Bitter." Now in 4:14–15, these same women bless the Lord on her behalf and ask a blessing on her and her family. What would you say is the significance of this faith community in her life? Why is the community important?

3 Do you have a community that can observe and bless God's work in your life? If so, what difference does that make to you? If not, what difference might it make?

4 Ruth's son became an ancestor of King David (verses 17–21), the greatest of Israel's kings. He also then became an ancestor of Jesus (Matthew 1:1–6). What does this tell you about where Naomi's story fits into the bigger story of the whole Bible?

5 Naomi's story mattered in God's big story far more than she could possibly guess in her lifetime. Your story also matters in God's big story far more than you can see from where you sit. But what *do* you know about where you fit in God's big story of drawing people from all over the world to himself?

6 If you were to dream, what would you like to contribute to God's story?

Journal Time

Choose *one* of the following topics to journal about:

- What opportunity do you have to pour energy and love into someone else's life? What will that cost you? What do you think about that cost? What will be the benefits of offering yourself in that way? What obstacles do you face in doing that? How could you address those obstacles? How do you respond to the idea of helping others in the midst of what you are going through?
- How could you abide in Christ this week, day by day? What will that cost you? What will be the benefits? What resistance have you felt in the past when you have tried to take consistent, daily time with God? What resistance have you felt when you have tried to trust God? Do you think you have any unrealistic expectations about what it should feel like to connect with God on a regular basis? If so, what are they? How might God help you get past your resistance and expectations?
- How has your view of God changed over the course of this study? Who is God to you now? Is God someone you can go to with your pain, anger, confusion? Is he someone you want to be close to? Or do you still have doubts about God?

Whichever topic you choose, finish up by writing about this question:

- What will you do differently in your day-to-day life as a result of this reflection? Again, use extra paper if necessary.

PRAYER ACTIVITY

Abiding in Christ should be like breathing in and out. We inhale by spending time with God, letting him feed us with his words of encouragement, truth, beauty, and sometimes correction. We tell him everything that's on our minds, so that he can carry it. Then on the exhale, we go out into the world and pour his energy and love into others. We take time to let him meet our needs, and then we take time to give ourselves to others' needs.

Give yourself ten minutes to talk with God about this in-and-out process in your life. What are the parts that come naturally to you? What are the parts that don't? For instance, does reading the Bible feel like work that doesn't feed your soul? If so, ask God to show you what you should be reading and how. Maybe you need to take one scene or one teaching from the Gospel of Luke at a time and pray over it. Or one verse from a psalm. Is it hard for you to be honest with God in prayer about yourself? Is it hard for you to give some focused attention to praying for someone else, or perhaps you find it hard to put words to what you want to say? Tell God whatever is hard for you, and ask him to help you. Do you find yourself drained in pouring love into someone else, or are you so caught up in your difficulties that pouring love into someone else seems impossible? If so, tell God where you're stuck. Ask him to show you why you're finding yourself so drained and what you should do about it. If you're overwhelmed, ask him to show you one practical step of love you could take for one person. Whatever your strengths and weaknesses, take them to God and invite him to train you how to breathe him in and breathe out love to others.

About the Authors

Nicole Johnson, Dramatist and Author

A bestselling author, performer, and motivational speaker, Nicole is one of the most sought-after creative communicators in America today. Her unique ability to blend humor with compassion, as she captures the inner most feelings of women facing life's daily struggles, has enabled her to create a unique sense of community for women of all ages. Nicole has twenty years' experience as an actor, television host, and producer, and has published eight books and a variety of curricula regarding relationships. She has written and performed sketches for the Women of Faith Conferences and written and directed dramas for The Revolve Tour. For three years, she wrote and performed dramatic sketches with relationship expert Dr. Gary Smalley, bringing her unique perspective to his seminars.

Jada Edwards, Bible Teacher, Speaker, Author

Jada Edwards is an author, speaker, Bible teacher, and mentor. Studying and teaching the Bible to women is one of her greatest passions, along with discipleship and living on mission. While she is a lively and sought-after speaker, the local church is her home. She and her husband, Conway, planted One Community Church in Plano, TX, where she leads a regular women's Bible study and serves as the Creative Services Director and Women's Director. Jada enjoys spending time with Conway and their two children, Joah and Chloe, particularly around the dinner table.

Kasey Van Norman, Author, Bible Teacher, Counselor

Kasey is a bestselling author, licensed psychotherapist and trauma specialist, and Bible teacher in Bryan, Texas. Alongside her husband, Justin, and their two children, Emma Grace and Lake, Kasey passionately serves her community at the Made Well House—a non-profit wellness center offering a holistic approach to healthcare through professional providers working in collaboration and grounded in a biblical worldview. Kasey has published two bestselling books with Bible studies, *Named by God* and *Raw Faith*. Kasey teaches and writes about the love that redeemed her life from the shame of past abuse, addiction, infidelity, and the fear of a life-threatening cancer diagnosis. She has spoken to thousands of women as a ministry event speaker—a headliner with the Extraordinary Women Conferences and American Association of Christian Counselors, and as an ambassador with Compassion International. Learn more at madewellhouse.com.

ALSO BY JADA EDWARDS

BEAUTIFUL WORD GALATIANS

Liberating Freedom is Found in Christ's Acceptance

In this six-session video Bible study, Jada Edwards will walk you through Galatians where Paul is giving a very passionate and urgent assurance, helping you understand that once you place faith in Jesus, you are transformed. You are made new. You are forever a part of the family of God. You are fully accepted, and you are free.

BEAUTIFUL WORD ROMANS

The Gospel is Our Lens for Life

In this eight-session video Bible study, Bible teacher Jada Edwards brings the clarity that we need for what the gospel is and how we live it out. Jada explores Paul's articulation of our faith and what it looks like in practice: how we love people, how we make decisions, how we submit to authority, how we live in community, and how we foster unity.

ALSO BY KASEY VAN NORMAN

NOTHING WASTED

Do You Wonder What God Can Do with Your Broken Past?

In this six-session video Bible study, bestselling author and speaker Kasey Van Norman offers a vulnerable exposition of just how capable and willing God is to resurrect us from sin and redeem us from all shame. Kasey takes the pressure off of outing our past, revealing God as the perfecter of everything that brings us shame or pain. God does not care if we are the reason for or the recipient of our messes–he uses everything to transform us. Nothing is wasted with God!

From the Publisher

GREAT STUDIES

ARE EVEN BETTER WHEN THEY'RE SHARED!

Help others find this study:

- Post a review at your favorite online bookseller.
- Post a picture on a social media account and share why you enjoyed it.
- Send a note to a friend who would also love it—or, better yet, go through it with them.

Thanks for helping others grow their faith!